CLOSING THE LOOP

PATRICIA WEINZAPFEL

HAWLEY
STREET
PUBLISHING
—— FOUNDED 2021 ——

PRAISE FOR *CLOSING THE LOOP*

"Effectively communicating with families and creating pathways for meaningful two-way communication is absolutely necessary if we wish to engage them in the learning lives of their children. To improve spoken and written communication with families and to set the stage for real and meaningful engagement, understanding how, when, where, and why to communicate is absolutely essential.

In *Closing the Loop, A Powerful and Practical Guide to School-Home Communication,* communications expert Patricia Weinzapfel, a trusted and authoritative voice in the field of communication, shares a proven pathway to inspire effective communication with every family and provides multiple opportunities to reflect, examine and improve present practice.

I have not seen a better or more compelling resource for educators looking to elevate communication and ultimately the engagement of every family."

—Dr. Steve Constantino

Nationally Recognized Family Engagement Expert and Best-Selling Author
Executive Professor, William & Mary School of Education

"Patricia's book breaks down the building blocks of great communication to help us all learn how to use clear, concise, effective language that will build relationships with families. Pair that with user-friendly technology, well, that can fundamentally change the school-home relationship."

—Gary Hensley

CEO and President, LivingTree School Communication Platform

"Patricia Weinzapfel provides readers with a timely, current perspective for removing the communication barriers commonly known to educators and families. Through awareness, implementation of simple strategies, and self-reflection, practitioners will learn to value each person's role in the development of the learner, creating powerful networks of support."

—K-12 Assistant Principal and Curriculum Coordinator

"Patricia strongly advocates for family engagement ensuring families are always on our minds and considered when new initiatives are developed and implemented. The contributions to family engagement and the strategies she shared have been helpful to us when consulting with other districts."

—Trish Hatch

PhD., Best-selling Author, White House Advisor in School Counseling and Department of Education Consultant

---

"Parents are the experts on their children. Teachers are the experts on teaching and growing children, socially, emotionally, behaviorally, and academically in the school setting. Schools and districts are experts on providing resources. In order to provide our children with the most suitable learning environment, tools, resources, approaches, etc., COMMUNICATION between the three is paramount."

—Karen Weiss

Award-winning Teacher

Download Activities and Checklists for FREE!

As a thank-you for buying this book, you can access a collection of blank activities and simple checklists you can use for free!

To download, simply focus your camera on this QR code.

It will take you right to my site.

CL SING
THE
LOOP

Activities and Checklists

Published by:
Hawley Street Publishing
Evansville, Indiana

If you're interested in learning more or working with Patricia, visit her
website, patriciaweinzapfel.com.

Because of the dynamic nature of the internet, any web address or
link cited in this book may have changed since publication and
may no longer be valid.

Photo by: Daniel Knight, Studio B Photography

Cover and book design: Wendy Hudgins, wendyhudgins.com

ISBN 978-1-7378431-0-8

First Edition

Library of Congress Control Number: 2022900084

Printed in the United States of America

For information about purchasing this book for business or
promotional use, or for special sales and quantity discounts,
please contact hawleypublishing@gmail.com.

For all of you amazing educators out there:
It is perhaps a cliché to say, but you are doing
the most important work in the world.
It's because of you that we always have
Hope.

For all of you incredible parents and
caregivers out there: Your strong advocacy,
fierce support, and intense passion for
your children are inspiring. It's because
of you that we can literally see
Love.

For my family, friends, mentors, and teachers:
Each of you has changed my life and left
a mark on my heart. It's because of you
that I continue to work toward my
Dreams.

TABLE OF CONTENTS

Chapter 4 The Building Blocks of Conversational Style

Chapter 5 Sharing Information: It's a Two-Way Street

Chapter 6 The Nuances of Tone and Body Language

Chapter 7 Challenging Conversations

Chapter 8 Dishing Out Data

Chapter 9 Making Good on Closing the Communication Loop

Chapter 10 Putting It All Together

Chapter 11 Ideas on Where to Begin

Chapter 12 Conclusion

References

i

ACKNOWLEDGMENTS

This book, or rather the idea for this book, would never have happened without Dr. Cathlin Gray. Cathy, thank you for taking me for coffee that October afternoon, allowing me the opportunity to reenter the workforce, and opening my eyes to a new career in the world of education. You are a mentor, a teacher, a friend, a big sister, and a great audience for my one-liners. Your support for this endeavor, your respect for this work, and your faith in me have meant more than I can express in words. You have changed my life.

Dr. David Smith, thank you for allowing me to be a part of your team for ten years and for giving me the opportunity to serve the children and families in our community. It was a privilege to come to work each day to a job that was so meaningful.

To the team at the Evansville Vanderburgh School Corporation, you are the most hardworking group of people I've ever met, and your passion for doing what's best for kids is infectious.

Thank you to all my friends and colleagues who took the time to read and edit this. I hope each of you sees yourself and your contributions in this final piece.

Thank you to my editor, Elizabeth Taggart, for your insight and work, my designer, Wendy Hudgins, for your creativity and passion, and to the team at IBJ Publishing for their help with the first iteration of this book.

To my parents, Alan and Dorothy Klineman: you have shown unwavering support, encouragement, and faith in me through all stages of my life. Thank you for engaging in my education, teaching me to work hard, and for instilling in me the desire to give back to our world.

To my children, Nathaniel, Benjamin, and Eleanor: it's a privilege to be your mother. I delight in each of you and in the love we share as a family. I now understand what my mom meant when she used to say, "I love you so much my belly hurts."

To my rescue dogs, Addy and Archie, you both say more without words than most people do with words, and your spirits, and love for life inspire me every day.

And finally, thank you to my husband, Jonathan. Your belief in me kept me going. I cherish the life we have created and crafted together and love you more with each passing year.

ABOUT THE AUTHOR

Patricia Weinzapfel is the founder and CEO of a consulting firm specializing in school-home communication and community collaboration. She works with school districts and organizations across the nation to help build bridges and partnerships that improve the lives of children and families in their communities.

Patricia recently retired from the Evansville, Indiana Vanderburgh School Corporation after spending ten years in administration for the district. In her role as the Executive Director of Community Schools and Family Engagement, she helped oversee the implementation of the community-school model and directed the EVSC's family engagement work in the district and its 40 schools.

Patricia holds two degrees from the Medill School of Journalism at Northwestern University: a Bachelor of Science in Journalism and Social Psychology, and a Master of Science in Broadcast Journalism with a concentration in Economic and Business Reporting. Prior to becoming a part of the world of education, Patricia got her start as a writer and producer for WSBT-TV in South Bend, Indiana. She spent four years as an on-air reporter at WFIE-TV in Evansville, was a special projects producer and writer for WTHR-TV in Indianapolis, and taught broadcast journalism and writing at the University of Southern Indiana.

Patricia served for eight years as First Lady of Evansville, alongside her husband, former Evansville Mayor Jonathan Weinzapfel. She partnered with several organizations on city initiatives and currently volunteers and serves on the boards of many nonprofits in her community, including the YMCA of Southwestern Indiana, the Committee to Promote Respect in Schools, and WFIE-TV's Advisory Board. Patricia has received recognition for her civic contributions, including a Junior League of Evansville Community Volunteer Award and a Chamber of Commerce Athena Award nomination.

Most recently, Patricia co-founded Read Evansville, a collaboration designed to prevent pandemic learning loss by providing new books to students. She also serves on the Greater Evansville COVID-19 Response Fund Allocation Committee.

Through the years, Patricia has honed her multitasking skills as a mother to three children—Nathaniel and twins, Benjamin and Eleanor—born less than two years apart. Patricia credits her rescue dogs, Addy and Archie, with helping her find the calm in her busy life.

PREFACE

This isn't a book about research. It isn't a book designed to use survey results or data to convince you that reaching out to families is important. Chances are, if you're reading this book, you already know that.

And it isn't a book to teach you how to organize a family literacy night. There are plenty of books that do that.

This book is designed with one purpose in mind: to help you improve your ability to communicate and build relationships with families. It's designed to help you use words and language to provide them with the skills and knowledge they need to become true partners in their children's education. It's designed to help you close the communication loop between home and school so that both you and your families are exchanging information and knowledge in a cycle that flows, builds, and grows.

While some people are naturals at communicating and others are not, all of us can learn to write and speak more effectively. These are skills that can be taught; you only have to recognize the need and be open to learning.

Developing your communication skills will help you not only reach out to families, but also to the community and to community partners working with students and families in your school. Many times they don't understand the world of education, either.

A quick note: In this book, I use the word "parents" in order to keep things short and simple. But the word "parents" is also meant to encompass caregivers, grandparents, foster parents, and other adults who love and take care of children.

Many of the examples included in this book were pulled directly from actual school and school district websites.

AUTHOR'S NOTE

I spent more than a decade immersed in the world of pre-K-12 education, working as a district administrator in family engagement. Along the way in my education career, I learned so much about teaching and learning, the education system, and how important it is to engage and partner with families. Today, I can talk the talk of an educator and hold my own, but I also bring an interesting perspective to the conversation. You see, I am not an educator by training. I'm a broadcast journalist. I am wired to observe things as an outsider, and this book is a result of that. It combines my two careers as an expert in pre-K-12 education-family engagement and an expert in journalism.

When I first found myself working in education, I never imagined I would end up writing a book. But as part of my job with my school district, I started attending community school and family engagement conferences, meetings, and forums.

Time and time again, I found myself sitting through breakout sessions where someone would lament the fact that educators talk in acronyms and use complicated language. I'm not kidding; it usually happened at least once in every session.

I listened and kept listening until finally, at one of the sessions, I looked around the room and thought to myself, *I don't know as much about education as these folks, but I do know about communication and I can help with this. I can help coach people on how to communicate better.*

And I started writing that night, in my hotel room while still at a conference.

This book took five years to complete. I stuck with it, in between raising three children, caring for my parents, and working full-time because, honestly, I felt compelled to write it. This is my small contribution to the world of education. I hope you like it. More importantly, I hope it helps you as you undertake the most powerful and important work in the world, educating children.

Why It's Important to Close the Communication Loop

Read this:

> *As a requirement of our CAP, EERC, and PBIS, Indiana staff will be visiting our district to attend a DLT meeting in the coming months. The agenda for the DLT meeting will, at minimum, include a review of CAP, root cause analysis, and any relevant data, as well as the needed resources and support from the EERC and PBIS Indiana.*

Did you really read it? Or did the first sentence just make you think, *No way?* Believe it or not, I actually received this email. I'd been working for a local school district for about nine months. When I opened the email, I took one look at it and thought, *Uh . . . not right now.* After I got myself focused with a cup of coffee, I actually read it. And then read it again. Finally, I called the person who sent it and said, "I'm happy to help in any way I can, but I have no idea what you're talking about."

You see, before I started working for the school district, I was a broadcast news reporter. My job was to take a complicated, confusing issue like "combined water-sewer overflow" and communicate it using words people could understand, in ways that would engage them in the information and make them *want* to understand. I was hired by my school district to help the staff work on communicating better with one another and with families.

Today, I completely understand that email because I now have ten years as a school administrator under my belt. I've developed an expertise in education. But at the time, I was still learning the school "biz" and didn't quite speak the language. In fact, in the first few months of my job in education, I Googled acronyms on my phone under the table during meetings and made lists of complicated words I didn't understand. And sometimes after meetings, I went into my boss's office and asked her, "What the heck just happened in there?"

Part of being a journalist is the ability to see things from an outside perspective. From where I sit now, with one foot in the world of communication and the other foot in the world of education, it's clear to me that we educators have our own language. At times, we like to talk really "smart." We use big words like "formative" and "differentiation." And we throw acronyms around like they're one-liners.

Lots of fields and businesses have their own specialized language, too. In television news, producers call live interviews between an anchor in a studio and someone in a different location a "jack in the box." In retail, advertised specials designed to entice you into the store are sometimes called "loss leaders." Turning background information into dialogue in a sitcom is called "laying pipe." This coded language is actually helpful. It streamlines communication because everyone in the business knows exactly what everyone is talking about.

The big difference is that those businesses don't use those terms when they work with their sources, consumers or customers (imagine telling the president of the United States that they are a "jack in the box"). In education, we often use our jargon and our smart, "fancy" way of talking when we communicate with families. That creates a barrier that doesn't allow us to reach out and engage them in true partnerships built on respect and centered on student success.

Here's a great example of what I'm talking about: In 2012, the Indiana Department of Education composed a letter for school districts to mail out to parents about the standardized reading test that all third graders take in Indiana.

Here's the letter's text:

In March, our school administered the Indiana Reading and Evaluation Determination (IREAD-3). Based on the Indiana Academic Standards, IREAD-3 is a summative assessment that was developed in accordance with Public Law 109, which requires the evaluation of foundational reading skills for students in grade three to ensure that all students can read proficiently before moving on to grade four. The result of your child's test is included.

Heck of a second sentence, huh? The letter goes on:

Your child's IREAD-3 score is:
☐ *Pass*
☐ *Did not Pass*
☐ *Undetermined (Contact school for more information)*

Questions may include identifying beginning, middle, and ending sounds, identifying synonyms, antonyms, homographs, suffixes, and using context clues to determine the meaning of unknown words in a text.

Here's how the letter ends:

If your child did not pass IREAD-3, our school will offer remediation services prior to the summer administration of IREAD-3. Details regarding the summer administration will be forthcoming. Should you need further explanation of the enclosed test results, please contact your child's teacher.

Let's start by asking which parts of the letter parents will understand.

The answer is easy: Probably not any of it. "Summative assessment," "foundational reading skills," and "homographs" are not words most of us use in everyday life.

Next question, what do parents need to understand?

They need to understand *all* of it if they are going to partner with us to help their children become strong readers.

Now, what part of this letter empowers parents to work with the school? What part of this letter is reassuring or friendly?

See, it isn't just the disconnect in the language or words. The tone and delivery also make this letter rather cold. It's sterile. It also has an authoritative feel that can be very intimidating for some parents.

The first step in building any partnership or relationship is communication. In other words, before we can begin to have respectful, meaningful conversations with families, they need to understand what we're talking about. We've got to be able to explain the complicated world of education without using complicated language. And that's harder to do than it sounds.

Sure, for some people it's just natural. And you know these people. They make it look easy. They could, as they say, "talk to a doorknob." But educators are often not so great at communicating with families. It's not all on them . . . they often haven't had any formal training in communication and they don't necessarily share the same cultural background of many of the families of their students.

However, educators have lots of strengths to build on. For one, most educators are gifted when it comes to communicating with children. So look at it this way: it's time to add to—or expand—your communication portfolio.

Here's the thing. You're already doing the work. You're already sending home the standardized test results, and you're already presenting to parents at your open house. This is just your opportunity to raise the bar. Because even though you sent the test results home, there's a good chance many parents don't understand them. And maybe those blank looks you got during your open house presentation aren't just because Mom, Grandma, or Dad are tired. Maybe it's because their overtaxed brains are working hard trying to decode what you're saying. In either case, parents don't necessarily end up with the information they need to help their children succeed.

So many other things can make communicating with parents uncomfortable . . . things like cultural differences, emotions, past experiences, age. If you can increase your ability in at least this one area—that is, choosing the right words, the right tone, the right message—you and your parents will have one less thing to worry about and you can be better focused on building relationships.

Choosing the right words, the right tone, and the right message seems so simple. It's really just talking, right? Something we do every single day, all day long. Most of the time words come out of our mouths, we don't even think about them.

They're just in the brain and then rolling off our tongues, almost instantaneously. Really, we usually stop to think about conversations we've had only when we think we've said something offensive, when we've had a particularly emotional exchange, or when we think we said something really clever or handled something well—or just the opposite—when we think of something clever we *could* have said.

The same is true about emails and other written communications. We don't have much time, so we usually don't take much time to finesse our Facebook posts or read over our emails to make sure they make sense, convey the right tone, and contain useful information.

That's okay in our everyday lives. No one wants to spend all their time replaying conversations or rereading emails. But in our work life, every exchange we have with our parents and caregivers is like gold, a precious opportunity to build a relationship that can make a difference in the life of a child.

Okay, that's a very "get-in-touch-with-your-feelings" way of looking at your role as an educator, so let's look from a more pragmatic angle at why it's so important to communicate with families in an understandable way.

INFORMATION IS POWER

To put it as simply as possible, parents and caregivers have information we need. When students walk into our classrooms, they don't come in as blank slates, ready to be filled up with knowledge. They have histories. They have strengths and weaknesses, likes and dislikes, and attitudes and personalities, all of which can factor into how successful students will be in our classrooms. And who better to tell us those things than parents? Parents are truly the keepers of the knowledge that we need to help students succeed.

Parents Are the Experts When It Comes to Their Children

When I give presentations, I often say, "I'm not an expert in algebra, but I am an expert in Benjamin Weinzapfel." All of our parents are experts, but we don't always look at them that way. Talking with them, and more importantly, listening to them, can help us understand the children we're trying to teach. In Benjamin's case, I've known that kid since before he was born, and I can tell you, when it comes to motivating him, "free dress" isn't going to cut it. But an extra trip to the library will. That's the kind of information that you, as an educator, need about a child. It's information that will make your job easier and make you more successful at keeping Benjamin motivated.

Sometimes the information is simple. Teachers are always surprised when I share that Benjamin is a twin, and that he and his sister, Eleanor, are a full year younger than most of their classmates. You can literally see the "that-explains-it" look on the teachers' faces.

Other times, the information is a little more complex and sensitive. I spoke with a parent once who called to tell me her daughter had not passed the statewide reading assessment. The parent told me she didn't know how to tell her daughter that she didn't pass. You see, her daughter always appeared to be self-confident in class, but in reality, the little girl struggled with self-esteem issues.

This was information that the little girl's teacher absolutely needed to know. I encouraged the parent to reach out to the school and share her concerns. Eventually, she and the teacher sat down together to talk with the student. The teacher was able to offer information, ongoing support, and encouragement, and the parent was able to bring her expertise about her daughter to the table in a powerful way.

At the beginning of sixth grade, my son Nathaniel's middle school teacher asked all the parents in the class to write a one-page letter about their children. The task was so simple, but so powerful. It was the first time any teacher had ever asked me to do something like that.

It was a joy to put together that letter. I felt like my opinion was important, and I felt like the teacher really wanted to know my son. But more than anything, I felt like an expert, like a partner, like I had something to say, something to contribute. Later, when my son had some issues in the class, I knew that the teacher and I could work together to solve them.

The sharing doesn't have to come in a letter, it can happen in a conversation, but the key is to recognize that all parents have expertise.

Parents Are the Experts When It Comes to Their Families' Cultures

Our parents also bring information about their individual family cultures and expectations. This is huge. We've always known it was important, but increasingly, we as educators are recognizing and talking more and more about the fact that what happens at home affects what happens at school. In fact, growing research suggests that how well children do at school is dependent on what happens outside of the school door, whether it is at home or in the wider community.

And we won't know what happens outside the school doors, unless we've taken the time to get to know our families. When we do, we get a much more complete picture of the children we teach. We begin to understand both the pressures and the challenges our students face at home and in the neighborhood. If we know, for example, that a student in our class is a first-generation American, we can better tailor what we say and do to support him and his family. We can better support, guide, and teach to the "whole child" who is our student.

This "parent voice," this knowledge our parents have about their children and their families and their cultures, needs to be at the table when we have discussions about our students. Notice that I said "parent voice." Ideally, parents are sitting right next to you when you're in a discussion. But even if time or scheduling doesn't allow them to attend a meeting, if you have previously reached out to that family, if you have talked and listened to them, you can bring the knowledge they've shared with you to the table.

The thing is, parents may not offer up their information if we have not taken the time to intentionally communicate and build relationships.

Families Can Change Our Assumptions and Help Us Become Better Teachers

When we genuinely talk with parents, really communicate, we might find out that the assumptions we made about them, both "good" and "bad," aren't true; and they might find out that assumptions they made about us aren't true, either.

We all do it. We all make assumptions about other people. In my early years as a reporter, I often found myself making assumptions about people I interviewed. I'm not going to lie, I was always respectful, but I judged people based on what town they were from, what kind of work they did, and how they looked. And you know what? When I dug a little deeper, I usually found that my assumptions were wrong. My experiences as a reporter opened my mind.

A few years ago, I was volunteering at a health-and-beauty back-to-school event. I was paired up with one of the school's volunteers. We were very different people with very different experiences. If we had assumptions about each other based on how we looked, where we worked, or other superficial things, we didn't acknowledge those. Instead, we focused on our volunteer work and, in the process, we started talking. Wouldn't you know it, we ended up chatting nonstop and completely hit it off. I had not doubted her commitment to her kids and the school, but at the end of our three-hour shift, I left with an understanding of her, of her background, of her beliefs, of her skills and talents, and of her hopes and dreams for her kids. It enriched my work. Even today, when I see her, that connection is still there.

When I'm out working with schools, the biggest assumption I hear from educators is that parents don't care.

Yet, if you sit down and talk with any parent, you will find that's almost never, ever the case. Sure, there are some parents who struggle with mental health issues or addictions, but by and large, those parents care, too. They may bring a variety of skill sets to the table, or they may have their own baggage from their school years, but they do the best they can when it comes to their kids.

Here's a little story about the "families-don't-care" assumption that I heard from an elementary teacher a few years ago. Let's call the teacher Mrs. Jones.

Mrs. Jones taught kindergarten, and a boy in her class was late to class every day. As you can imagine, Mrs. Jones found that awfully frustrating. She assumed that since the boy's mother was young and lived in a poor neighborhood, she just didn't care.

Mrs. Jones ended up taking part in a home visit program set up by the school. She had a chance to sit down and talk with this young mother in her home, on her turf, in a relaxed, friendly setting. There was no "you must do this," or "why don't you do this?". The two just shared their hopes and dreams for the child. Mrs. Jones then learned something that shook her assumptions and changed her student's life.

It turned out that each morning, this young mother was right outside the school door in plenty of time for her little boy to make it to class . . . but bless his heart, he just couldn't walk in. Mrs. Jones learned that the little boy had anxiety. His mother would plead, beg, bribe, offer extra kisses. Each morning, she did everything she could to get him to go through the door, and he just couldn't do it. Once Mrs. Jones learned this, she and the mom worked together to help the little boy. He began seeing the school counselor. And Mrs. Jones started meeting him at the door. Now he walks right in. Mom feels more comfortable, too. And now Mrs. Jones replaces assumptions with phone calls and home visits.

Good Communication Can Help Build Education Equity

For some families, school-home communication is just fine. They get it. They understand all the words, they have the time and the experience needed to sit down and process all the information, and they have the confidence to navigate the school world and advocate for their children.

But this isn't the case for all families. And in order to create an equitable educational system, all families should have information they need, presented in way they can understand.

In 2015, Congress passed the Every Student Succeeds Act, the main education law for public schools in the United States. The law holds schools accountable for how students learn and achieve, and it aims to provide an equal opportunity for under-resourced students, including those who get special education.

The language spells out the need for effective two-way communication. And, it specifically speaks to the need for information to be presented *"in an understandable and uniform format, and to the extent practicable, in a language that family members can understand."*

This is intended to make sure that all English language documents are translated for families who speak other languages. But think about it, the words we use and the way we often write and speak can make it difficult for even our English-speaking families to be a part of the education process. One other thing to keep in mind . . . well-written, well-presented communications translate easier into other languages. In other words, it's tough to translate a word like "fluency."

Families Can "Shop" for Schools

We live in the era of school choice and school vouchers. There are lots of good school options out there for parents and that means there's competition. Families can take their children anywhere. And sometimes, if parents and caregivers don't feel you understand them, respect them or want to partner, they will.

Private schools have faced this issue for years. In fact, many private schools hire marketing firms to help them communicate with families, and those schools put time and effort into designing communication plans. They often work with their staff to help build their communication skills. As a result, many of these schools' teachers and other staff are really good at listening and partnering with parents. In some ways, they might feel like they have to be. After all, parents are often literally paying their salaries.

But those of us in public schools aren't used to the idea that we need to market our services. More and more public schools are hiring PR staff and that's all great and good, but in the end, public relations and marketing campaigns can't make up for poor communication. If you reach out, listen, and connect, then in many ways you're providing both good marketing and good family engagement by closing the communication loop.

Engaging Families Is Part of Our Evaluations

Education laws are changing, and in many ways, *this is the moment* for family and community engagement.

The changes mean there are more opportunities for parents to be involved in decision-making about education at the local and state levels. At the same time, schools and school districts are being held more and more accountable for their plans and their ability to engage and partner with families.

At the heart of all of this is effective relationship building, engagement, and communication.

In many instances, the quality of a teacher's communications with families are included in teacher evaluations which factor into promotions and raises.

For example, in the Massachusetts Standards and Indicators of Effective Teaching Practices' "Family and Community Engagement" section, teachers are measured on their ability to "engage in regular two-way communication" and to practice "culturally proficient communication."

As we say in the world of education, what gets measured gets done; and some districts and teachers are feeling the pressure that now is the time to just "do it," but they still don't quite know how.

BARRIERS TO COMMUNICATING WITH FAMILIES

The world of education and teaching has become increasingly complex. Schools are constantly evaluating students to check for learning. Teachers are using technology and software to tailor instruction, and they are working to help students grow not only academically, but also socially. Some schools are even incorporating mindfulness and physical activity into their teaching day. Some of the changes are a result of legislation; other changes have grown out of recent brain research.

All of it is a far cry from the good ol' one-room schoolhouse. And all of it is a lot for parents to understand. Classrooms today are far different from what they remember. So it's on us to figure out how to package information and talk about what's happening in the classroom in a way that's digestible and understandable, and in a way that engages our parents.

Parents and Families Are Busy

Before I started working in family engagement for the district, I was a parent with children at one of my district's elementary schools. One day after I picked up my kids, I was going through the mail and saw a letter from the superintendent. I remember opening it, looking at it, and thinking, *I know I need to read this letter, but I can't do it.* It simply looked too long. Could I have read it? Yes . . . absolutely. But that would have required some time, and I didn't have the time, especially at that moment. I needed quick, easily accessible information. The same is true for our parents. As educators, we need to understand that oftentimes our parents can't devote lots of time to reading our communications. We need to convey what we need to convey quickly.

The letter I received probably had important information, but it was written with lots of big, complicated words. Even if it had been shorter, just a quick look at the language would have told me that it would require my full attention. I'd need to really think as I read it. I'd need to really focus. And with three young kids, dinner on the stove, and doctors' appointments to book, I already had enough things competing for my attention. I needed easy-to-read and easy-to-understand information.

I'm not trying to say that parents don't have a responsibility to read over what we send them or to call us back. I am saying we need to make it as simple and easy as possible for them to do so.

When you think about this idea of having time and devoting attention, it's the reason some of us read *USA Today* and not *The New York Times*. It's the reason for the success of Twitter.

I never read that letter. I thought I'd get to it that evening after the kids went to bed, but I never did. I think it ended up in the garbage. Reading the letter right then and there, when I first opened it, was the only opportunity the school had to reach me. *Time and attention.* They really boil down to the fact that you may have only one chance to communicate something important, and you don't want to waste it.

Schools Can Be Overwhelming or Scary for Some Parents and Caregivers

You may be thinking, *I'm around, I'm available, parents can call or email me anytime. After all, communication is a two-way street.* And you're right. It is. But the responsibility for the exchange of information rests first with us because the fact is, for many of our parents, it's really hard to step foot into a school.

Parents can feel intimidated for lots of reasons. Some parents did not have good experiences in school, and they don't really want to go back there. Perhaps they didn't graduate, perhaps they didn't get along with the school staff or a teacher, or maybe they were bullied. They bring those experiences with them, and those experiences shape their perspective and their actions. For me (and if you're in education, you're probably like me), when I walk into a school, there's a spring in my step. It smells like a school, there are books and pencils, and it brings back such great memories. There's a warm and fuzzy feeling because I was successful in school. But for many parents, school doesn't evoke pleasant memories.

Parents sometimes stay away because they don't feel respected. They already feel that their opinions and voices aren't needed, or even wanted. Maybe they pushed into the school, tried to talk with a teacher or staff member, and felt as though they weren't treated like an equal partner. So why bother?

This happened to me. The first day I dropped off my son, Nathaniel, for kindergarten, I walked him to his classroom, gave him a big kiss and hug, and handed him off to the teacher. It was as if I were leaving my heart in her care. The next day, I started down the school hallway only to be told, "You can walk him to class only the first day." I was stunned. How would I know how he did? How would I talk with the teacher? How would I know what to ask him about on the way home?

I never questioned the school. I got the message. You're great, but we'll take it from here. That didn't make me feel like a respected partner. You know what would have made me feel like a respected partner? If someone had explained *why* I couldn't walk my child to class. I might have still been disappointed, but I would have understood that it was good for my son.

Other parents stay away because they don't have confidence, and they don't want to "screw it up" for their kids. For others, schools can seem very institutional and very complicated. They view teachers as experts, and as parents, they don't think that they have much to contribute, or even that they *can* contribute. They may not send emails or call for fear of sounding stupid.

I know a little bit about how that feels, too. When I was interviewing for my position with the school district, I took a tour of one of our middle schools. The principal walked me down a hallway and we peeked into a classroom. She said, "The students are composing music on their netbooks." Let me set the stage: I was coming off ten years at home with my kids. I didn't even know what Microsoft Outlook was, and here these kids were using computers in a way I couldn't imagine. I was literally sick to my stomach at the idea of what I didn't know and the idea that I wasn't capable of helping my own kids. I thought, *I gotta get out of here.* It was completely intimidating, and honestly, I felt awful about myself and my abilities.

Communicating with parents and caregivers can help remove many of the "ghosts" in the classroom and help build up parents' confidence. It allows us to share information with parents in a respectful way that can result in student success—and not just information about academics. Some teachers say that knowing their students' parents is the only behavioral strategy they need.

FAMILIES CAN BE OUR MOST POWERFUL PARTNERS

All of the research is clear: family engagement is the greatest predictor of student success. Research shows that regardless of family income or background, students with involved parents are more likely to earn high grades and test scores, enroll in higher-level programs, be promoted, pass their classes and earn credits, attend school regularly, have better social skills, and graduate and go onto postsecondary education.

Studies also show that parents of all income levels and ethnicities want to be involved in their child's learning and they want information, even if they don't attend bake sales or call the school.

And get this: research even shows teachers are happier when parents are engaged.

That's why communication matters. If we want our students to succeed, we've got to build the relationships with their parents that support information sharing and learning.

A WORD ABOUT THE COVID-19 PANDEMIC

In many ways, when it comes to engaging families in education, COVID-19 changed everything. The pandemic highlighted just how important it is to bring families into the learning process. It exposed weaknesses we can now work on when it comes to our communication practices with families. And it brought home the importance of truly understanding and acknowledging that education is a shared endeavor between schools and families.

But one of the biggest things the pandemic did was create a lot of good will and mutual respect between families and educators. For the first time, many teachers were reaching out to their families in ways they had never done before. They were calling to check on families, doing home visits to connect with students and, through virtual teaching, they were actually "seeing" the inside of many of their students' homes. This gave teachers a true understanding of what families face, and a true understanding of just how much families want their students to succeed. At the same time, families were getting more than a glimpse of just what goes into teaching these days. And for the first time, many of them developed true respect for the special people who choose to go into teaching.

A national survey of families during the pandemic by *Learning Heroes* showed many families have recommitted themselves to seeking out a better understanding of school work and their child's progress.

The pandemic has given us a window of opportunity. It opened the lines of communication. Families are ready to engage. And with the right training and support, we can keep those lines open and work with our families to help students succeed.

If we didn't know it then, we know it now. Communicating with families isn't just nice, it's absolutely necessary.

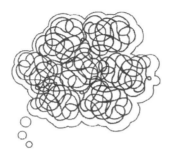

Why We Can't Close the Communication Loop

"Language is a beautiful thing."

That's what my dad used to say to me when I would go to him looking for advice. "Use your words," he would say, "and if you're honest and choose the 'right words,' you can handle most anything." It's true, there's rarely something that can't be made better with an apology, a lighthearted quip, or a loving expression.

Words are tools. We can use them to build bridges, forge compromises, and mend fences. And they are powerful. Just think about when you're having a lousy day. One kind word, perhaps from the cashier at Walmart, can sometimes change everything.

Most of us do realize the strength in what we say and in the words we use, if only because with our words, we encourage our children, negotiate with our mates, and comfort our friends. So why don't we approach reaching out to our students' families the same way? Why don't we always put more thought into our words, our conversations, and our communications with parents?

BARRIERS TO COMMUNICATION

There are lots and lots of barriers to good, effective communication. Sometimes those barriers are simple . . . let's say you had a lousy day and don't feel like talking. Or your shoulder hurts, or you're mentally preparing yourself to help your own child with schoolwork when you get home. Or maybe, you are deep into the conversation with a student's parents, but you're simply thinking more about how you'll respond, than truly listening to them. Barriers like these exist in our world of education and families, and the first place to start to remove them is by creating the right conditions for your conversations to take place. Let's look at some of these barriers to open, productive, and family-friendly communication.

The Time Trap

Many educators say the biggest reason they don't communicate well is time. We know we need to reach out to families, we know we need to explain what we're working on in class, but there's just not enough time to pick up the phone or send an email. And even when we do see a parent by chance, perhaps in a hallway or at school pick-up or drop-off, a million other things are usually going on at the moment—we're headed to monitor study hall, or prevent a kid from stepping off a curb in front of a bus(!). In the busy world we live in, it's hard to be present and "in the moment," and frankly, it's hard to remember that the time we spend on our letter or email will really, truly help families work with their children. It's hard to remember that small pleasantries we exchange with parents really do matter and can have a huge effect.

The Need for "Know How"

We don't always close the communication loop as educators because sometimes we just don't know how. It's that simple. It's a very rare teacher-training program that includes any training on communicating with families (or communication, in general). In fact, a *Harvard Family Research Project* and *National PTA* issue brief on preparing educators cited research showing that many universities include family engagement courses in their teacher education, but that all too often, the courses are only designed around early childhood or special education. This research also showed that teacher education programs continue to face serious challenges in incorporating family engagement into the curriculum, including inadequate systemic support and limited resources.

It's no wonder then that teachers say they enter the classroom unprepared to engage families, even as they acknowledge lack of support from parents as their most pressing challenge. Teachers may have the skills to see that Johnny is struggling in math, but they don't have the skills to build relationships and engage families in a conversation around how to work together to help Johnny.

In many ways, teachers must develop the skills to communicate on the job, and that can be difficult because there is limited professional development, and frankly the skills don't always come intuitively. But you may already know this, because you're reading this book.

Lack of Desire

Let's face it. It can be hard to be in education these days. Really hard. It's an especially trying time for teachers. They sometimes have it coming at them from all directions. Honestly, I don't know how they—how *you*—do it. Changes in technology, data, accountability, curriculum, standardized tests, discipline, class size, continuing education requirements, compensation . . . the list could go on and on, and it can all add up to lots of stress and leave teachers feeling discouraged, skeptical, even grumpy. Intellectually, we may know family engagement works, but all this negativity can make it harder to step back and really trust that making the effort to talk or reach out to parents or putting extra effort into that newsletter is worth it. No doubt, for many overwhelmed teachers, it seems like just one more thing they have to do in the sea of other 'have-tos.' The point is, parents pick up on that. And it doesn't make for sunshine and roses.

The Teacher/Authority Mindset

Even if we have the time and the training needed to communicate and we want to follow through with it, it's hard sometimes for us to shift our mindsets. We've been teachers all day. We've had to speak as the expert or act as an authority figure. We've had to corral kids, we've had to be in charge and on duty, and we've had to command respect and enforce rules and expectations.

This approach works well in the classroom, but many teachers find it hard to switch from a commanding tone and adopt a partnership approach when talking with parents. In other words, we sometimes want to continue our lecturing or teaching when we interact with parents, when what we really need to do is listen, and help them understand and navigate the world of education.

The following draft of a letter is an example of where we try to be welcoming, but can't get out of the teaching mode and the use of complicated, formal language.

Dear Parents/Guardians:

We are excited to share that we will be implementing the PSAT 8/9 to a subset of our 8th grade students this spring. These students were selected based on their strong academic records. Your child was one of those selected! The PSAT 8/9 tests the same skills and knowledge as the PSAT/NMSQT in a way that is appropriate for 8th grade. This assessment establishes a baseline of college and career readiness as students enter high school and provides valuable information to plan and guide the student beyond high school into postsecondary education.

The PSAT is the preparatory test for the SAT. All sophomores and juniors take the PSAT/NMSQT, which is paid for by the state. The junior year PSAT/NMSQT is the National Merit Scholarship Qualifying Test. While it is not required that your 8th grader take the PSAT, statistics do substantiate that the more practice a student can do for the test, the better the scores will be. The College Board's most recent research indicates that on average students who take the PSAT prior to their junior year score 3.5 points higher on each section of the PSAT and that students who take the PSAT score 145 points higher on the SAT. Additionally, every student who participates in the PSAT has access to a program called My College QuickStart, a free resource that lets students use PSAT scores to predict SAT scores, go over questions they got wrong on the test, see a list of recommended colleges, and create a customized SAT study plan.

It is our hope that you will allow your child to take the PSAT 8/9 with the other selected students at Martricia Middle School. There is no make-up testing for the PSAT.

Please return the permission form below to have your student register for the test no later than January 15, 2017. If you have questions, feel free to call or email [CONTACT].

Sincerely,
The Administration Team

Here the letter gets a makeover.

Dear Parents/Caregivers,

Congratulations! We have chosen your child to be a part of a group of students we feel have the skills and abilities needed to get a head start toward college.

As part of applying to college, your child will be taking an exam called the PSAT. The PSAT is usually offered to sophomores and juniors, but we feel your child is ready to take a version of the test this spring.

Taking the PSAT early has its benefits. It's good practice for your child. In fact, research shows the more times your child takes the PSAT, the higher your child will score on important college entrance exams like the SAT.

There are other benefits as well. The information we will get from the PSAT will help us provide what your child needs to plan for his or her future. Plus, taking the test will give you and your child access to free resources that will help as your child begins to look at college.

We will be offering the PSAT at Martricia Middle School on March 3.

Your child will not need to prepare for the test, but will have to attend school that day. There's no make-up exam.

Your child is not required to take the PSAT early, but we sincerely hope you will allow your child to take part in this opportunity.

Please return the permission form below to your school. There is no charge for the test, and we will take care of registering your child. If you have questions or concerns, please call XXXX.

Thank you, and thank you for all you do to help your child succeed!

Sincerely,
XXXX, Principal

The second version of the letter conveys information in a way that doesn't come across like teaching, but more like *sharing*.

Beyond the Education Bubble

Say what you will, but from my perspective, as someone who came in from the "outside," the world of education can be a big bubble. You know how it goes: you're a teacher, your dad was a teacher, your husband's a principal, your best friend's the school counselor . . . it happens naturally. But these can often be the folks we interact with the most—other educators. It can be challenging to spend time with people outside the world of education. It can be even more challenging to spend time with the families of the children we teach.

In broadcasting, we call this "separateness." In some ways, it's encouraged. Journalists shouldn't become too attached to a community or the people they are covering for fear of losing objectivity. But in the case of teachers, becoming more attached to the world outside of education can actually help us by allowing us to understand how the concepts, and the words we are using to explain them, are being received and, more importantly, understood by our parents.

In the education bubble, people use big words and acronyms. What's the language you hear all day around school and in your classroom? It's ISTEP this, and DIBELS that, and words like summative, assess, and fluency. When those are the words you hear day in and day out, you tend to use them. You read those words, over and over, and that way of communicating becomes entrenched in your brain. With the people we work with or educators we socialize with, those words are more efficient. We all know what summative means, and we can say all that it means in just one word, instead of five. But with families, this approach actually makes conversations less efficient and less effective. We almost waste our breath using those types of words. They hinder real communication and true understanding.

Those big words can also help us "sound smart," like educators are supposed to be, right? And let's be totally honest here, some people do like sounding smart. There's power in feeling like you have mastered something. We use that language not only because it's the language we use, but also because it impresses others and makes us feel good about ourselves. Once we've experienced that kind of power, it's hard to let it go.

After a few months with a foot in the education "bubble," I found myself fighting to stay away from complicated educational words. It's especially hard when people ask me what I do. But honestly, using those words and those acronyms is just off-putting for everyone involved, not just families, but also community members and partners, anyone outside the education bubble. Even now, I'll slip up and use a term like"embed," and when I do, I feel the need to apologize and say, "I really don't like using words like that."

A trip outside the bubble can be eye-opening. For years, the school district where I worked marketed the parent grade-checking system by calling it "Ed Ease." But that's not what teachers called it. They were used to referring to the grade system, both the teacher- and parent-facing sides, by the name of the operating system, a series of initials, let's call it, "ABC." That was the name they used with other teachers, so naturally, they used the same name with parents.

Once we stepped outside the bubble, we saw how confusing this inconsistency was for our parents. We were asking them to check Ed Ease, and teachers were asking them to check ABC. We couldn't change how the teachers referred to it; they weren't going to call it one thing with parents and another with each other. So we changed the name to "ABC Parent Access." This phrase incorporated both the system and what teachers said, while also better describing what it was. I don't *love* the word access, but it's better than what we had.

Here's another great "outside-the-bubble" story. Within the grade-checking system, there's a page where parents can check standardized test scores. One day, we were working with a parent on the system, and she was so happy to log on and see that her daughter had a "B" on the test. She thought it meant a "B" like on a grading scale of A to F. She didn't know that B actually meant "Below Passing." We realized then that we needed to step outside the bubble, shift our perspective, and make some changes to the system to help parents understand.

Stepping out of the bubble is one of the keys to good communication. It's really about stepping outside your experience and your knowledge level and into the experiences and knowledge levels of your families. When you do that, you can see and understand how and what you need to communicate.

It takes effort and it takes desire to get out of the bubble. A few years ago, I worked with a committee of journalists and writers. We put together easy, understandable ways to explain the tests and assessments schools use with students. We approached the project like reporters—the academic folks were our sources for information—and then we took the complicated language and, as one of the writers put it, "gave it some love." When we got the draft to the point where we were comfortable, we sent it back to the academic team for a final review just to make sure our translations into "regular people"-speak were accurate. The review proved to be anything but final. The academic team must have spent an entire day rewriting the draft, reinserting words like differentiation and predictive and using a very authoritative tone. Eventually, we were able to adopt the more family-friendly version, but not without some difficult conversations. For some, the education bubble can be hard to pop.

Don't Just Check It Off

I hear this from other educators a lot:

"The newsletters went out; I communicated."
"I posted the grades to the portal; I communicated."
"I sent home the parent compact for a signature; I communicated."

I call this the "checklist approach" to school-home communication. Educators feel like they've communicated and engaged families if they've ticked off the list of required communications. But communication is defined as an interchange of thoughts, opinions, and information. It's a two-way process of reaching mutual understanding, and creating and sharing meaning. And the checklist approach is a one-way communication pushing out information; it won't help us build the relationships with families that we need to get to true communication and true engagement, and it won't help you close that school-home communication loop. Don't get me wrong, these "to-do" tasks keeping parents informed are important. But we have to strive for communication that moves beyond the checklist approach to meaningful understanding.

It's the Law!

In some instances, we're told to use our complicated terms and language. Many times, state law will require schools to send home letters or forms that do not set a partnership-friendly tone. The folks who draft these documents suffer from the same challenges that the rest of the education world faces, but with a little government red tape thrown in. Legislators are not educators, are not communicators . . . you get the picture. Even if state law requires that we send home certain information, we can still repackage it, even if this means including a cover letter for the cover letter to the document.

Believing in Our Families

Sometimes we can underestimate what our parents are capable of comprehending. We have to remember that all parents can understand education information as long as that information is communicated in an understandable and compelling way.

This is big: We've got to believe in our families. Research shows they want to help their children. And research shows they are craving the information to do just that.

A recent survey from the *National School Public Relations Association* found that parents want information on what their child is expected to learn, their child's progress and how they can improve, along with timely notices when their child is struggling. They are also looking for information on homework and grading policies, and descriptions and details about instructional programs.

Now think about what we often share with parents. It's information on the uniform policy, the sports scores, or the date of the dance. Parents want and deserve more. They deserve information delivered in a way that matters to them, in a way that is convenient for them, and in words they can understand.

I was at a meeting once where I handed out some data to parents and caregivers on just how many of them were checking their children's grades online. A grandmother raising her grandson and another parent from one of our more under-resourced neighborhoods looked over the numbers and had a little discussion. "Wonder why more parents were checking in March?" said the grandmother. And the other parent said, "Well, that's I-STEP and I-READ (standardized testing) time, so maybe that's why." Together they figured out that the uptick in parents' checking was tied to the standardized testing window. How cool is that?

Really, parents will get it; they want to. If we present our messages in clear, concise ways, they will understand. And they will be able to join us in the true partnership that we're looking for, one that will result in good things for kids.

The Scare Factor

Let's get real for a second. It can be scary to pick up the phone and call someone you don't know. Or someone who doesn't look like you or share your experiences. It's even harder when the information you need to share is challenging. So what do we do? Well, sometimes we just avoid making those calls. Or we avoid sending home that email, or having that family-student conference.

I get it. When I was a reporter, I had to make calls to all of the police agencies in our area to see if there was any "spot news" . . . crime, fires, accidents, etc., that we needed to include in our newscast. When I first started out, I was so nervous,

I could barely speak my name and remember the call letters to our TV station. In time, I got into a rhythm. I grew comfortable making those calls, and even got to the point where I'd chitchat with the dispatcher on the other end of the phone. But it was hard in the beginning. I don't know if I would have stuck it out if it wasn't my job. Bottom line, it takes practice to get comfortable at communicating, but it is possible.

We Have to Listen . . . and Change

When we finally, truly communicate with families in ways that are meaningful and respectful . . . well then, we have to listen to what they have to say. And that means, we may have to change. We may have to change something we're doing, a program we started, or a bus route. And change can be hard.

But if we really value families, and we believe that education is a partnership, we owe it to our families to not only hear their thoughts, opinions and ideas, but incorporate them into our education process. In the end, that will make for a stronger education system. One that works for and *with* families instead of against them.

One thing to always keep in mind: families won't tell you if they don't understand something. They won't tell you if they feel overwhelmed with information. And they won't tell you if they feel intimidated or disrespected or shut out of the process. They will simply disengage. We won't see them and we won't hear from them. The responsibility for preventing this disengagement lies with us and our ability to close that communication loop.

I'm a huge fan of "you need to know where you are in order to figure out where you need to go." The first step in becoming good at communicating with families is to understand where we are and why we do what we do. Then we can start the real work of using language to create, in my father's words, "a beautiful thing" for our students and their families.

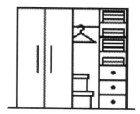

A "Wardrobe" of Writing and Speaking Styles

So you're taking some time, you're stepping out of your bubble, and if you've made it this far, you're a believer. On behalf of your students and families, thank you! Sincerely.

Now let's get started. First, let's take a look at different styles of communicating.

You do it automatically, but each time you speak, write, and communicate, you're sizing up your audience, and making assumptions about what kind of language or gestures are appropriate for the person and the situation.

When we talk about styles of communicating, we're talking about more than grammar and punctuation and more than rules for speaking or writing. In *The Elements of Style*, William Strunk Jr. and E. B. White write, "The rules are about what a writer does; style is about how the writer does it."

To break it down in an even more simple way: style is really just the way you choose to communicate to your audience. It's the words you use, the voice you use, the tone you use, and the way you organize your thoughts.

Here's how it works. You sit down to write a quick email to your sister:

Jane,
The book is in the mail. You should receive it on Wednesday.

But after writing the text, you think about it and add:

Jane,
I am so superexcited to send you the book! You will love it! I
dropped it in the mail last week . . . should get to you by Wednesday.

The first email, maybe a little too businesslike for a sister, might leave her wondering if you meant to send the email to her. The second email is a little more appropriate for someone you brushed your teeth next to every morning for years.

Here's another example of differing styles, this time with body language. You walk up to a business colleague who you really know and respect, and you feel like giving the person a hug, but in the split second before you do, you size up the situation, decide a handshake is better, and avoid that awkward handshake/hug thing that sometimes happens.

In this instance, you opted for a more business-like greeting. Even if you're friends with your business colleague, and you, yourself, are a hugger, a hug has the potential to send the wrong message or be misinterpreted.

When you choose a communication style, you need to think about not only who your audience is, but also what your goal is. Just as you wear different outfits for different occasions, you can choose from three 'wardrobe' styles of communication for different situations: formal, technical, and conversational.

FORMAL STYLE: THE SUIT AND TIE

Think about the most recent research paper or educational journal article you worked your way through (because likely it took a lot of effort). That research paper was probably written in a very formal way, in part to reflect what the author thinks is the seriousness of the work. There were probably long words, lots of "who-did-what-to-whom" passive voice writing, and lots of clauses, phrases, and commas. Lots of commas.

This is a more formal style of communicating, the way your English teacher taught you to write. When writing in a formal style, you follow all the grammar, punctuation, and spelling rules. Formal style uses longer, more complex sentences and perhaps bigger, more precise words coded for a highly specific audience. It is intended to be objective; the writer is not emotional, and there's a sense of the writer being outside the information. Formal language does not use contractions, colloquialisms, or first person pronouns such as "I" and "we," and most often uses "one" rather than "you."

Formal style serves an important purpose. It is the accepted form of communication in many business situations and in many academic worlds. Formal style is also used for more official presentations and situations, such as lectures and ceremonial addresses.

It's important to recognize formal style and its rules of communication so you can break, or at least bend, those rules when you reach out to parents.

TECHNICAL STYLE: WORK CLOTHES

Now go and pick up the manual to your coffee maker or microwave and take a look at it. That "how to" booklet is also communicating information but in a technical style. That technical style is designed to be authoritative, but also clear and concise so you can actually read the manual and operate the microwave. No long phrases here; just "flip the red button up," and so on.

Technical style is efficient and is used to give directions, instructions, or explanations about how something works. Technical style is clear, impersonal, and opinion-free. (But how much fun would it be if it wasn't? *When you push this microwave's On button, you're in for a real treat!*) It's also free of emotion. After all, you're not trying to build a relationship with your coffee maker.

Technical writing serves an important purpose. It's not about the reader or the audience. It's not about entertaining or encouraging the reader to think, and it's not about building a relationship with the reader. Its sole purpose is simply to convey information and instruction.

CONVERSATIONAL STYLE: CASUAL FRIDAYS

When we communicate with our families, we want to use what's called conversational style. It's also the style we use in broadcast journalism and increasingly in print journalism and on the web. To put it simply, we want to communicate the way we talk. That means using simple words and simple sentences.

You read material that's written in conversational style all the time in blogs, articles, and social media posts. You can recognize conversational style because that's what it is, conversational. When you read it, it's as though the writer is speaking to you. So the writer uses contractions, short sentences, and colloquial phrases. Conversational style interjects emotion, extra words, and pronouns like "we," "you," and "I."

We use conversational style because it's more welcoming. It's not pretentious, it's not fussy, it's not formal, and it's not complicated. It draws you in, just as a good conversationalist draws you in.

We also use it because it helps us build relationships. When you're communicating with parents, you're not delivering a speech, you're not lecturing a class, you're not telling folks how to turn on their microwaves. And you're not writing a research paper for all your fellow educators. You're reaching out to build an equal partnership.

There's a lot of powerful neuroscience research on the effectiveness of conversational style that shows that it works because it tricks the brain into thinking it's in a real conversation. And what happens during a conversation? Your brain pays attention because it thinks it might have to respond.

You might be thinking, *Now, that shouldn't be so hard, right? I can talk, so this conversational style should be pretty easy for me.*

Yes and no.

Remember, in our work lives, we're not necessarily speaking conversationally, and actually it's very, very challenging to take complex ideas and communicate them in simple, understandable ways.

When it happens, it's magic, and it can seem effortless. Good conversational style is good because it doesn't call attention to itself. All that's conveyed is the idea and the information; the words just fade away. To put it another way, the language is not so formal or flowery that you notice it. You won't think, *Wow, that writing is terrific!* Or, *What a great way to phrase that!*

Conversational style is easy to read and listen to. You don't have to concentrate so much to get the message. Like oatmeal, it's easy to digest while still being meaningful.

Conversational style is not so complex that you tune out, that you stop reading or stop listening. Above all else, good conversational style gets across the messages that you hope to share in a way that is clear and to the point.

Think Mary Higgins Clark versus Jane Austen. I'll admit. I've never made it through Jane Austen. I couldn't put forth that much effort. I just saw the movies. However, I've been known to enjoy a Mary Higgins Clark novel a time or two. They don't ask anything of me. And from what I remember of Jane Austen's writing, it is rich with details, but so is Mary Higgins Clark's. Two different writing styles, two different periods of literature, and two different audiences with different expectations.

Let me make one thing clear. When we use conversational style, we're not dumbing down our communication because we're not dumbing down the information. It's as complex as ever; we're simply conveying it in a way that is understandable.

You can be the smartest person in the world, with the best idea in the world, with a complex innovation that will change the world, but if you can't communicate it to others so that they understand it, your idea will go nowhere. Oh, maybe some other highly educated colleague will get your drift, but I bet even that person would rather not have to work so hard to understand you. The point is, conversational style works with everyone, from someone whose background you know nothing about to your most notable colleague.

I've written federal grant reports. I've written grant applications. I can write in business style, I can write in technical style, and I can talk all day about PLCs, PBISs, and functional behavior analysis. But I don't like to. I believe the world would be a better place if we were all able to understand what we were all talking about. If doctors used regular language, how much more engaged would we be in our health? How much more would we understand them? If human resources staff took the time to really explain our benefits in a way we could understand, how much more engaged would we be in our finances? And if, as educators, we improved our communication style by using plain language, how much more engaged would our parents be in their children's educations? How much more would we be able to help our students with their parents' involvement and how much more could we learn from them?

Here's an example of copy from a school website that's written in a very formal way. When you read it, notice the big words, the lack of emotion, and the long sentences. And keep in mind that this might form a first impression for families interested in sending their students to this school.

Welcome to Martricia School

Martricia School operates under the paradigm that every child is capable, and every child is a leader. The school's vision, excellence in developing the whole child, is exemplified in the many collaborations with PTA and the community to bring experiences to teachers and students that enrich the opportunities available. The school's mission, to collaborate to create leaders, empower learners, and ensure growth, guides our decisions and our direction. Incorporating this mission in all decisions helps develop the essential life skills and characteristics students need in order to thrive in the 21st century. This approach sets the foundation for children with personal leadership and equips students with the self-confidence and skills needed to thrive in school and beyond. Additionally, the school differentiates instruction to meet the needs of all learners. Small group reading instruction is implemented school wide, and the math workshop model is offered in some grades. Students from Martricia will attend Hamilton Middle School for grades six through eight, then move on to Jefferson High School.

Now, check out this rewrite of that same website copy. When you look it over, notice the conversational style . . . the short, snappy sentences, the simple words, and the emotion. Think about the first impression this sends to families.

Welcome to our Martricia Family!

Thank you for enrolling your child in Martricia School! We are excited to work with you to make sure your child succeeds here!

Our goal at Martricia is to nurture and challenge each of our students so they become lifelong learners and strong, confident leaders.

At Martricia, we believe that education is a partnership and we know you are an "expert" when it comes to your child. We hope you will share your ideas and expertise with us. We want to hear from you. And we will reach out often to let you know how your child is doing

We'd love for you to take part in school events and activities at Martricia like Family Reading Night and our PTA. We also encourage you to take advantage of resources at the school. We can work with you to not only meet your child's needs, but your family's needs, as well.

Again, thank you for choosing Martricia. We look forward to standing alongside you and sharing in your child's success in the years ahead.

Sincerely,
Anne White, Principal

Some of the information in the passages is a bit different, but both speak to the focus on leadership, lifelong learning, and family involvement in PTA using different words and styles. One is formal, the other is conversational. Big difference.

Honestly, I'd argue that conversational style is the most effective form of *any* communication. Why? Because when you use conversational style, your reader (or listener, for that matter) doesn't have to put any effort into understanding your message. It's easy and it connects, and in this day and age with all that's vying for our time and attention, and with the complexity of information we're being asked to understand, we all need the easiest way to connect.

Remember, it's the simple, easy messages that get through. If I have to struggle to read something or listen to something, I won't. And I don't think you will either. It's probably part of the reason you haven't put this book down yet.

The Building Blocks
of Conversational Style

In the chapters ahead, I will talk about both writing and speaking. But do understand that if you can write in conversational style, you'll naturally begin to speak in a very conversational way, and vice versa. You will catch yourself when you start to use acronyms and complicated language, and before too long you'll begin applying conversational style to conversations. Imagine that!

CONVERSATIONAL STYLE TIPS

Let's just get it out there . . . there are conversations, and then there are conversations. When you're talking with a teacher in the breakroom about the latest lesson you're writing, or working in a PLC (Professional Learning Community)—going over your LDA (Locally Developed Assessments)—you're having conversations, but you're not necessarily talking in a way that will draw parents in, so it's not quite as simple as writing the way you talk.

It's sometimes hard to break down just what makes up conversational style, but here are some of the guiding principles and tips that can help.

Don't Use a Five-Dollar Word When a Fifty-Cent Word Will Work

I once had a journalism colleague who would often quote from Mark Twain: "Don't use a five-dollar word when a fifty-cent word will work." In other words, don't use complicated, big, or fussy language if you don't need to.

In education, there are a couple of terms for five-dollar words that you might have heard before—"educationese" and "edutalk." Whatever you call it, speaking or writing, you don't want to use them.

The words you use when you communicate with families should be simple—as simple as possible. I mean, if you're using lots of multi-syllable words, especially in one sentence, consider that a huge red flag. If you have a choice between a simple word and a more complex one, always choose the simple one.

In broadcasting, I was always taught to aim to use words that could be understood by fourth to sixth graders. Simple words. Plain language. But even in broadcasting, you still hear five-dollar words. Reporters use "purchase" when "buy" is a better word; they feel the need to use "laceration" for "cut" and "contusion" for "bruise." I don't know why. It's not good.

Here are some other quick, common examples from the world of broadcast journalism. Now that I'm pointing them out to you, you'll probably hear them everywhere.

State law mandates	State law says
Currently	Right now
Reside	Live
Unsure	Not sure
Utilize	Use
Sufficient	Okay
Accumulate	Gather
Participate	Take part
Demonstrate	Show
Assist	Help

You get the idea. Can you see why it's not so easy to just "write the way you talk"? If we use these words in speech, we will tend to use them when we write. Education is full of five-dollar words. And sometimes it's not easy to replace them with just one word. So it's okay to use lots of little fifty-cent words to replace the big five-dollar word. You'll still come out ahead. Think of it as an investment in relationships. I promise, you will not run out of words.

Here are some of the five-dollar education "All Stars" and some quick translations:

Assessment .... Test
Retained...................................... Remembered
Retained...................................... Held back
Data .... Information
Proficiency .... Skill
Differentiated.............................. Tailored

In some instances, it will take a few fifty-cent words to explain certain terms, which is okay, too.

Fluency .... Reading words without stopping
                                                            and starting
Predictive assessment .... Test that tells us how your child
                                                            might do
Differentiated instruction............. Learning customized or tailored
                                                            to your child
Assessment.................................. Test that helps us see where your
                                                            child is with his learning
Summative assessment................. Test that compares your child's
                                                            understanding and knowledge
                                                            based on what we hope your child
                                                            will learn
Formative assessment................... Test that helps us know where
                                                            your child is with their learning
                                                            so we can better teach your child
Academic standards .... What the state expects your
                                                            student will know and be able to
                                                            do at the end of a grade
Curriculum.................................. Teaching materials

Do you see how it works? It's almost like decoding something.

I will never forget . . . early in my job, the district needed to adopt a new reading curriculum. The language arts specialist asked me to bring together (notice how I avoided the word "assemble") a group of parents to review the books and materials. I rounded up a very diverse group of parents, caregivers, and grandparents and pulled together the meeting. All of the participants sat and listened as the language arts specialist started talking about the books. She began by talking about the fact that all the books needed to meet the state academic standards for the grade level. At the mention of the word "standards," I watched as many of the participants started to fidget and sink lower into their chairs. I finally raised my hand and asked, "Can you explain what standards are?" The language arts specialist looked surprised. But once the specialist explained what standards are, the parents, caregivers and grandparents perked up and they were "all in" with the work. They needed to understand the language before they could take part in the conversation about the curriculum.

I have worked in education for ten years. But I still come across five-dollar words I don't understand. On one Southwestern school district's website, I found a blurb on the district's gifted program and found myself, once again, Googling words.

SUSD Gifted Programs provide challenging curriculum to gifted students through the use of differentiated instruction designed to best meet the academic and affective needs of the students. The gifted program is designed to teach students with meaningful learning experiences that foster an enriched and in-depth understanding of the core curriculum. These best practices for gifted education guide and shape our gifted programs throughout the district.

Curriculum, differentiated, affective, foster . . . this is just full of five-dollar words, plus it uses the good old "best practices" term that we educators use all the time. I promise, my mom friends and I have never used the term "best practices" in conversations about our kids.

One thing to note . . . and we addressed this in Chapter 1, we don't want to make assumptions about our parents one way or the other. There are many parents who might understand everything in the passage above. But what we want to do is make sure *all* parents can understand and be a part of the conversation.

Avoid A.C.R.O.N.Y.M.S.

I hesitate to write this. Because honestly, it's probably okay to use some acronyms, and I'll give you an example. Our statewide yearly performance assessment is called the Indiana Statewide Test of Educational Progress-Plus. If I said to a parent, "How did Susie do on the Indiana Statewide Test of Educational Progress-Plus?" that parent would have no idea what I was asking. The test has been around for more than ten years, and parents know it as ISTEP. It's kind of like PTA, or FBI, or CIA. It's okay to use acronyms when you're absolutely certain your audience will understand them. But before you use one, really think it through, think about your audience. If you do choose to use an acronym, always check for understanding by asking your families, "Do you know what those letters stand for?" One other thing to keep in mind: acronyms in this country stand for English words, so a non-native speaker might not understand even a common school acronym like PTA.

When you do use an acronym, you'll probably need to define it. And that doesn't mean just spelling out the words the letters stand for. Because if you tell a parent that a BIP is a "Behavior Intervention Plan," they still may not know what you're talking about. Instead, building on my example above, give them the letters and define the term. Say, "A BIP is a Behavior Intervention Plan, the plan we will work on together to make sure your child has the support and strategies they need to be successful." And here, again, don't forget to give a few examples of the supports or strategies you're talking about. "When your student has completed all of their assignments in class, they can have free time that includes things like computer time, napping, reading, or playing in the gym."

Here's another example of how to do this: "Your child will be taking an End-of-Course Assessment or ECA. This is the test we give at the end of the year that all students must pass in order to graduate with a high school diploma." Approaching it this way will help you be certain that parents fully understand the acronym.

But honestly, even if you're speaking to someone in the field, it's better to leave out acronyms. I had a woman from one of our state universities call me about coming down for an interview, and she kept referring to the "CCR and R." It probably took me fifteen minutes to remember that CCRR stands for Childcare Referral and Resource. That was fifteen minutes that my brain was not listening to her; instead, it was focused on running through the acronym dictionary in my mind. As a result, I missed some of what she said and it was hard for me to listen and participate in the conversation.

It's Okay, Use Contractions!

When we speak, we use contractions. They're conversational and concise. And they help tell a story or convey information in a fluid, uninterrupted way. To get an idea of what I mean, here's a suggestion from grammar.yourdictionary.com:

> *Record yourself when you are talking on the telephone and then transcribe your conversation. You will notice when you go back and read it that there is a definite conversational style. Once you see your conversational voice you will better be able to use it in your writing on demand.*

Contractions help you hear the voice in your head when you read. I always use contractions, but if you decide not to, just be aware that using the full words in place of contractions will "formalize" your language just a bit. Your communications will be less conversational, but you can still be concise and clear.

The Power of "You"

I'm a huge fan of the word "you." It gets people's attention, and it seems more personal. Let's face it, you're trying to break through the clutter of a giant attention-seeking world. When you call me out by saying, "Hey, you," I pay attention. My "you" fandom also spills over to "your" as in "your student," "your school," and "your child."

When you use "you," it also seems as if you really see me, you know me, and you recognize me; it makes me feel *special*. Think about the difference between "Parents will need to pick up their students in the cafeteria," versus "You will need to pick up your student in the cafeteria." It's informative, and in fact, both say the same thing, yet the second is more personal and friendly and more conversational.

A side note here: A study published in the *Journal of Educational Psychology* looked at the difference between informal and formal writing in learning. In all cases, students who learned with personalized text (using "you" language) did better on tests. The idea is that when you use "you," the brain somehow thinks it's involved in a conversation and therefore has to pay more attention to hold up its end. The brain thinks it's being talked *with*, not *to*. Think about our parent partners and let that idea digest for a second . . . interesting, huh? Don't we want to talk *with* them and not *to* them?

Have Just One Person in Mind

While you're writing or practicing your communications, try to think about communicating with just one person. This will help you think in terms of "you." And it will help you keep everything more informal and less like a presentation.

If you're writing or speaking to everyone, to all of your parents, you will end up sounding formal. You'll end up using phrases like "those of you" or "students" instead of "you" or "your child."

Here's a short example that might help explain what I'm talking about. It's from the website of a small Midwestern school district.

> *Louisville Public Schools CENSUS Registration*
> *Families residing in the Louisville Public School District (Cedar Creek, Louisville, South Bend) with children at the age of five and younger are encouraged to pre-register their child. [Click to Register]*

In this example, we're writing to *families,* not *a family.* We're also not writing to *you, the person reading the website.* Much stronger to write:

> *Louisville Public Schools CENSUS Registration*
> *Do you have children aged five or younger? Do you live in Cedar Creek, Louisville, or South Bend? If so, please click here to register your child for school!*

When you write or think about speaking to just one person, your message will be clearer and more effective.

Here's another example, but this one starts out speaking to everyone, then switches to speaking to one person, then goes back to speaking to everyone. It's from a school district in the Northeast.

> *Northampton Prevention Coalition would like to invite parents and students to come to the NHS cafeteria on Tuesday, March 28 from 5 to 6 p.m. for pizza and a brief talk by the Northampton Police Department and the District Attorney's Juvenile Court on the Social Host Law. If you have the "All Sports" meeting to attend at 6 p.m., let us feed you first while you learn how to*

*reduce the risks that can come with underage parties and drinking. This event
has been scheduled so participants can go to both meetings if they choose.*

Are you talking to me, are you not talking to me? It's not clear. This starts
out with "parents," switches to "you," and then ends with "participants." Better to
address this as if it is going to just one person.

*Northampton Prevention Coalition would like to invite you and your
student to come to the NHS cafeteria on Tuesday, March 28, from 5 to 6 p.m.
for pizza and a brief talk by the Northampton Police Department and the
District Attorney's Juvenile Court on the Social Host Law. If you have the
"All Sports" meeting to attend at 6 p.m., let us feed you first while you learn
how to reduce the risks that can come with underage parties and drinking.
This event has been scheduled so you can go to both meetings if you choose.*

There's a simple way to always ensure you're using "you." Think about what
you need to say or write, and then visualize telling this to a friend, neighbor, or a
parent. Think of that parent sitting across from you drinking coffee, or sitting in
her kitchen reading email, and then write or speak to them.

The author Stephen King once said, "Write to your Ideal Reader. Aim at
everybody, you'll hit nobody. You'll be less focused than a puppy in a flurry of
tennis balls."

Use Simple Sentences

Research shows that your ear and your brain can generally digest one fact per
sentence. If you try to cram more than one fact into a sentence, your listener's ear
or reader's brain will react by tuning you out or losing interest. Your listener won't
have a chance to rewind the conversation, and you don't want your reader to have
to reread anything.

Here's a great example from an Indiana Department of Education website
page marketed to parents:

*Superintendent Glenda Ritz and the Hoosier Family of Readers
challenge classrooms throughout Indiana to celebrate the Indiana bicentennial
by reading 200 books, either digital or print, before December 31, 2016.*

Lots of facts and figures there in one long sentence. Go back and try reading this outloud to yourself. Did you have to take a breath in the middle? If so, it's most definitely not conversational!

Let's break down all the facts here:

> *Glenda Ritz and Hoosier Family of Readers*
> *Statewide*
> *Classrooms*
> *Challenge*
> *Celebrating the Indiana bicentennial*
> *Read 200 books*
> *Digital or print*
> *Deadline of December 31*

Time for a rewrite:

> *Students across Indiana can help celebrate the state's bicentennial . . .*
> *by reading books. Indiana's top educator, Superintendent Glenda Ritz, has*
> *challenged students across the state to read 200 books by the end of the year!*
> *The books can be digital or print. The challenge is sponsored by the Hoosier*
> *Family of Readers.*

Not perfect, but certainly more digestible. Now read this one out loud. See the difference?

By breaking the information into separate sentences and doing a little rewriting ("end of the year" versus "December 31, 2016"), you make the information more conversational and easier to understand. Think of it this way: you need to try to share information in bite-size pieces.

A few months ago, one of my colleagues pointed out that my emails were written like broadcast scripts. And they are. I don't really write in paragraphs. I write one fact per sentence, one fact per paragraph. The emails look a little odd, but they're easy to read and easy to digest. Plus, they look simple. How many emails do you open that look like term papers, so you don't read them? I would venture to say that that doesn't happen with mine. Even when they're long, they don't "look" long.

You don't have to write broadcast scripts, but do try to speak and write with a one-fact-per-sentence mindset.

Here are clues that you're overdoing it: You're using lots of commas. And lots of phrases. Try to reorganize your phrases as separate sentences.

Prep the Reader's Ear

Just as your ear and your brain can digest only about one fact per sentence, sometimes they also need to be *prepared* for what they're about to be told or what they're about to read.

You can do this by cueing readers or listeners in on what you're about to tell them. Here's an example:

> *There's been a change in the school's uniform policy.*

When I read or hear this, I'm prepared to read or hear what comes next. I'm now reading or listening for what that change is. Also, in the back of my mind, I'm thinking about the policy and refreshing my memory on what the policy includes right now. This is a very effective technique for putting information in context and preparing your audience. Going back to the "before" example about the Bicentennial Challenge:

> *Superintendent Glenda Ritz and the Hoosier Family of Readers*
> *challenge classrooms throughout Indiana to celebrate the Indiana bicentennial*
> *by reading 200 books, either digital or print, before December 31, 2016.*
> *Students across Indiana can help celebrate. . . ."*

In the "after" example, by putting the students up front in the sentence, we cut through the noise and prep the reader for the rest of it. After you read or hear the first sentence, you wonder, *How can they celebrate?* And you're listening in order to find the answer to that question. You're prepared to hear or read what comes next:

> *Students across Indiana can help celebrate the state's bicentennial . . .*
> *by reading books.*

Piece by Piece, the Logical Way

If you listen closely to a well-written news broadcast, you'll notice this. As a story moves along, information is presented in a logical way, the way the reader or listener will want to receive it.

This is effective, conversational story-telling. You paint an overall picture first and then ask yourself, *What will the reader or listener be asking at this point?* Then lay out another fact and again ask, *What's the reader or listener wondering now?*

Let's say that you're sending out information about a new reading assessment. Here's how it might go:

> *"This year we are using a new reading test to help us tailor our teaching to your child."*

Parent wonders: "What is the new test?"

> *"The new test is called DIBELS."*

Parent thinks: "DIBELS, that's a crazy word, what does it mean?"

> *"DIBELS, which stands for Dynamic Indicators of Basic Early Literacy Skills, is a test that tells you where your child stands in terms of reading, writing and math skills.*

Parent thinks: "How does it work?"

> *"Your student will take the DIBELS test online. It's a series of multiple choice questions."*

Parent wonders: "How often will my child take the test?"

> *"We will do DIBELS testing three times a year."*

Parent wonders: "How will it help?" And, the communication answers that question.

"We will know how your child did on their DIBELS test right away, and we can change our teaching strategies to make sure their learning is right on target!"

Parent thinks: "Sounds great, wonder how I can help?"

"You can help by making sure your child gets a good night's sleep and a healthy breakfast before they take the test."

Building your communications piece by piece—logically—will help you as you lay out information in a logical, understandable way.

When a communication isn't built piece by piece in a logical way, it can be very frustrating. Think about a time when you were listening to the radio and a story about an upcoming event was being talked about. As you listened, you thought, *Wow, that'd be fun to attend,* but by the time you figured out you'd want to go, by the time you heard the enticing details about the event, you'd already missed the information on where and when it would take place. That's because the where and when information probably came before the event details, as in this script of an automated phone message for parents:

The school is hosting a Literacy night September 9 at 7 p.m. The event will feature dinner, musical performances performed by the 5th grade class, and a community information fair. Come enjoy a meal, sign up for a library card, and learn about the state's Bicentennial Reading contest.

By the time you decide, *Wow, I need a library card*, you're thinking, *Wait . . . what . . . when?* The information has passed. Better and more logical:

The School is hosting a Literacy night. The event will feature dinner, musical performances from the 5th grade class, and a community information fair. Come enjoy a meal, sign up for a library card, and learn about the state's Bicentennial Reading contest. The "Literacy night" will be held at the school September 9 at 7 p.m.

In the second example, the information builds piece by piece. It's less likely to frustrate parents, and it's more effective communication.

The Dog Ate the Bone

You want to use the active voice as much as possible. Here's a quick refresher from your good old high school English days:

Active voice: The dog ate the bone.
Passive voice: The bone was eaten by the dog.

You can recognize passive voice because it generally uses a "to be" helper verb, such as "is," "was," "am," "were," "be," "has," "have," "been," and "will." You can also recognize it because the receiver of the action comes before the verb.

Active voice is more direct, so you use fewer words. It's straight to the point. And it's simple. And get this: it's also easier to digest because it's linear and logical. The subject does the action.

Passive is more clumsy and wordy because the subject of the sentence is acted upon. And it's less effective when communicating because it requires your mind to move stuff around. And that takes effort. You have to listen very closely and think about moving the noun back in front of the verb to get at the meaning of the sentence. Passive voice can also change the focus of sentences. In the active voice example, "the dog ate the bone," the focus is equally on the dog and the bone. In the sentence using the passive voice, "the bone was eaten by the dog," the focus is more on the bone than the dog.

Passive voice can sometimes lead to long, complicated sentences and can cause readers to lose interest, or become confused as they try to move all the words around in their heads.

People sometimes fall into the trap of using passive voice because they think it sounds more official:

"The test will be given."
"The legislation was developed."
"The grant was awarded."

It's much clearer to say:

"I will give the test."
"Your child's teacher will give the test."

Passive voice also doesn't make us assume responsibility for our actions. "Parents are asked to stay away from the school while the school is in secure mode," or "The doors to the school will be locked."

Instead, we write or say, "We are asking that you hold off on coming to the school when we are in secure mode," or "In order to keep your child safe, we will be locking the school doors." We don't pass the buck; we take responsibility for our actions. Also, it feels more "relationship-y" and less institutional.

In some instances, you can use passive voice, for example, if you're not sure who performed the action, or if you need to leave out who performed the action. Think about crime stories: "The store was robbed," or "The body was left in the bedroom." The subject (who robbed the store or left the body in the bedroom) is unknown.

Also, if you want to stress the receiver of the action, you might use passive voice: "The district was awarded a $5,000 grant from the state" seems stronger than "The state awarded a $5,000 grant to the district." In this instance, you want to focus on your district, not on the state.

You may use passive voice when the person doing the action isn't as important as other information in the sentence. For example, use "The high school's magazine recently received a designation of 'Excellence' from the National Council of Teachers of English program," instead of "The National Council of Teachers of English program recently awarded the high school's magazine the designation of 'Excellence.'" Or you could write, "The production will be presented July 15, 2015," instead of "The school will present the production July 15, 2015."

But generally with parents and caregivers, you want to use active voice because no audience effort is needed and there's no question about who's performing the action. Plus, active voice can help build the parent-school relationship.

Here are some quick tips on "fixing" your passive voice:

Relocate the actor of the sentence:
   A test has been given by the teacher.
   Better: *The teacher gave a test.*

Place the actor in the sentence:
   The test was given.
   Better: *The teacher gave the test.*

Change the verb:
> *The bell has been rung.*
> Better: *The school rang the bell.*

Keep in mind that one of the biggest reasons people don't listen or read what we communicate is time. Using passive voice lengthens whatever you're writing or saying because it requires more words. Look at the earlier example of the dog and the bone. The active voice used five words; the passive voice used seven. In terms of time and attention, shorter is better for everybody. Say what you need to say and move on.

Toss (Some) Grammar out of the Window

It's okay to lose the grammar rules, at least some of them. This may be tough for all you grammar police, and I get pushback all the time from educators on this one. When we speak, we start sentences with "And" and "But." We end sentences with prepositions. We pause when we speak. However, ditching some of our grammar rules in order to improve how we're communicating is perfect when we're having conversations with families. It makes us seem approachable and real.

We can do the same with our written communications. I'm not saying abandon grammar altogether, but don't make a sentence awkward in an attempt to follow "the rules." If there's a choice between formal grammar and conversational style, choose conversational style. If you really have a problem, work harder to rewrite your sentence so that it's short, conversational, *and* grammatically correct. Otherwise, don't sweat it, don't worry so much about being a rule follower.

I can hear all your arguments from here! I know, we're teachers; but in this instance, we're not trying to "teach" parents. We're trying to communicate with them.

So those are the basics. Sound easy? Maybe. But it's more challenging than you think because it's not as simple as following rules.

Here is a beautiful example of conversational style. It's a letter from a Chicago area public school district on its website explaining emergency closings…something that's pretty important for Chicago parents to understand during a polar vortex!

Dear Parents,

I'd like to give you a peek at how the District manages snow clearing and decision-making for the open/close of school.

First, you have found the District 39 "Emergency Closings" page. If you are ever unsure of whether schools will be open, you will find the most up-to-date information here. On bad weather days, we will update the link by 5:30 a.m.

Next, I want to share with you how we arrive at the decision to close our schools on a particular day. It is a fretful process that can begin the day before.

When the snow starts falling, I pull out my phone and click on the Weather Channel App (TWC Max). I check the forecast, the radar, and any posted advisories. I check it again . . . and again . . . and again. I keep a close eye on the approaching storm; all of this before bedtime! Then, at 4 a.m., I take a scientific "look out the window" and begin checking the Weather Channel yet again.

If I get an "all clear," I go back to bed!

Otherwise, I call Stan Stankiewicz, District 39's Director of Operations and Maintenance, who is already at work. He gives me an update of the salting/plowing progress at each District 39 building. I get ready for work and leave home by 4:30 a.m. On my way, I call the Village Public Works Department (the snow plow department) for local road conditions. In fact, I can even dial right into a snow plow! The driver can detail for me the status of street salting and snow clearing in the Village.

Next, I literally drive to the schools to get a feel for the conditions and identify any trouble spots. If I see any difficult driving areas, I call my friends at Public Works so they can address the concern.

Between 4:30 and 5:30 a.m., all school superintendents in New Trier Township telephone conference heavily about whether or not to close schools. We share all of the collective information we have. We want to make decisions as early as possible and the "drop dead" decision time is 5:30 a.m. As a group, the NT Township schools agree to make the same decision on bad weather days.

If a decision is made to close school, then communication with parents and staff begins. The most important part of that communication involves a call to you, letting you know that schools will be closed. Faculty and staff are also notified. At the same time, the website is updated and the media is informed. Please make sure to notify us if your phone number changes.

I hope this helps you understand the process that takes place so often during the winter months. Please let me know if you have any questions or concerns.

Thanks!

The letter is signed by the superintendent, who happens to hold a Ph.D. Don't you kind of like him? The conversational style makes you feel like he's talking to you. Not only talking to you, but telling you a story. You can't help but read it. Plus, it's respectful.

And now that you know just what all goes into closing a school, it makes you less likely to complain about the next snow day . . . which might have been the purpose of the letter in the first place!

I will leave you with one thought. David Ogilvy, considered in many ways to be the father of modern advertising, once said, "I don't know the rules of grammar . . . . If you're trying to persuade people to do something, or buy something, it seems to me you should use their language, the language they use every day, the language in which they think."

Sharing Information: It's a Two-Way Street

By definition, communication is a two-way activity. It's about imparting and exchanging ideas, thoughts, opinions, and information. This exchange implies that for communication to be successful, it's not enough that you say what you want to say in a way that's simple and understandable; it also means that the person you're trying to communicate with gets it. That is, real communication doesn't take place until the information has been received and processed by the person.

So here's my number one tip for deciding what information to share . . .

Know your audience.

That means, before you even start writing, and before you even sit down to have a conversation, it's important to step out of the education bubble and step into the shoes of your families. Spend some time just thinking about your parents and caregivers. What are their backgrounds and are those backgrounds different from yours? Where might they be emotionally? What are they concerned about? When might they receive your communication? Are they a captive audience, or are they focused on lots of other things? Questions like these will help determine what information to include and what information to leave out. If you know your audience you will naturally be able to decide what information is important to them.

Here are some suggestions to help guide you when it comes to sharing information.

THE DOS

Effective communication can be very subjective. It's like art, it's mainly in the eye of the beholder . . . or in our case, the brain and heart of our audience—our parents and caregivers.

But when it comes to information sharing, there are some keys to making it easier to prune your communication to the essential elements.

Do Tier Your Information

When it comes to what to communicate . . . here's my second biggest tip:

Share information according to the amount of detail your particular audience needs. Here's what I mean:

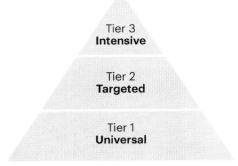

You may have seen a triangle like this before. It's used quite a bit to illustrate how schools provide support and differentiation for students. The idea is that at the bottom level, Tier 1, we are providing *universal* quality instruction for all students. Research shows that 80 percent of them will succeed with this level of quality instruction. Even with that high-quality instruction, research shows that 15 percent of the students will need a little extra support or a little more challenge. We put those students in Tier 2 . . . so we can provide targeted interventions or what they need to be successful. At the top level, Tier 3, research shows 5 percent of the students will need intensive, one-on-one support or wraparound services to be successful.

When we communicate with parents, we can take the same approach. At the universal level, our first tier, we can provide the minimal amount of quality information that all parents need to participate in the learning process. There will be parents who will want to know more, parents who have questions, or parents who will need a little more support or background information to understand how to support learning at home. We put these parents in our second tier. And finally, there will be parents that want to know tons of details (maybe they're going into teaching!), or parents we will need to work with one on one to bring about understanding. We can put these parents in our third tier.

Here's what our triangle looks like now:

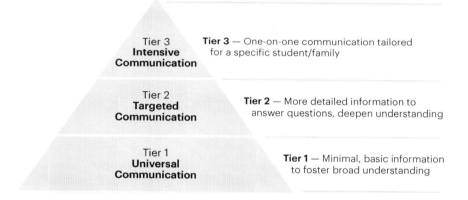

Tier 3
Intensive
Communication

Tier 3 — One-on-one communication tailored for a specific student/family

Tier 2
Targeted
Communication

Tier 2 — More detailed information to answer questions, deepen understanding

Tier 1
Universal
Communication

Tier 1 — Minimal, basic information to foster broad understanding

When you are communicating with parents, when you are deciding what information to include in your newsletter or your back-to-school presentation, and what information to leave out, you'll want to strive to communicate at the Tier 1 level. You'll want to provide the basic information that all parents need and can understand. That means you'll have to look at every detail and ask yourself: is this Tier 1 information or Tier 2 information? If you can provide basic—but quality—information in an understandable way right out of the gate, you will reach the majority of parents with what they need to support learning at home, and ensure that you're not providing too much information. And remember, basic doesn't mean impersonal or not conversational. Basic is still family-friendly and warm! And by approaching it this way, using Tiers 1, 2, and 3, you'll give families the information they need to ask questions or participate a little more deeply, and that will give you opportunities to build relationships.

Do Define Your Goal

All of your communications with parents should have a purpose and a goal. You can't begin writing or speaking unless you have some idea what you want to convey, and why it's worth conveying.

I taught a broadcast writing class at a local university for a few years. I used a technique with students to help teach this idea. I handed them a long article about a complex subject, gave them time to read it, and even take notes if they wanted to; then I asked them to put it away. Once they did, I asked the students to give me a one-sentence summary of the article. In many instances, it was difficult for students to cut through all of the details and words to find the purpose and goal of the communication.

Before you have your conversation, design your flyer, or send your written communication, come up with a one-sentence goal that captures the purpose of your communication. Your goal might be to inform parents about a new procedure at the school. Or it might be to persuade them of the benefits of joining the PTA. Or it might just simply be to get to know them better. But understanding the purpose can help you pare down your information to what is essential and make your communication more effective and efficient.

A word of caution . . . there is some flexibility to this. Remember, effective communication is a two-way process, so listening to parents, *really listening,* may mean that the conversation or communication will go in a completely different direction than you initially planned. And that's okay. You need to be a little loose. You may not fully achieve your one-sentence purpose, but you will still exchange information and cultivate a partnership.

It's kind of like when I was a reporter and went out to investigate a story. I usually had enough background information so that I had an idea about what kind of story I'd have when I returned to my office. But sometimes, when I actually got to the scene, the story went in a completely different direction. Instead of staying focused on the narrative in my head, I stopped and saw the story in front of me (which, by the way, was usually better than the one I had envisioned in my head).

Do Include "The Why"

When you give parents information, be sure to include the "the why." This goes back to the idea that education is a shared responsibility. If I, as a parent, understand why you're doing something the way you're doing it, or if I understand why you're asking me to do something, I'm more likely to trust you and support you.

Here are some great examples. I have a friend who is passionate about free play for children. She went to her son's school to discuss the fact that the students had only about ten minutes for free play during recess, and then had to spend ten minutes lining up in alphabetical order to go to lunch. And I say "to discuss," but honestly, she went in with a bit heavier approach and was a little confrontational. Her main point was, why couldn't the kids just line up and go in? That'd be quicker and allow more recess time than all the alphabetical stuff. To her, the alphabetical approach made no sense.

The principal's response was amazing. She acknowledged my friend's concern and then took the time to explain "the why." She told my friend that the children had to be in alphabetical order in the event that there was an emergency at the school. The teacher had to know that, after recess, all the students were accounted for. Wow! Makes perfect sense, and even my friend admitted that it wasn't a bad idea. In fact, once she understood the school's reasoning, she supported it.

Here's another example. In second grade, my son came home with a paper and said, "Mommy, you need to listen to me read this, and mark when I make a mistake." The instructions on the paper said to do that, too. So I did it. But I didn't know why I needed to do it, or exactly what I was supposed to be listening for. I now know it was an exercise to check his fluency—his ability to read without starting and stopping. If I had known that, not only could I have fully participated in that homework, but I could have incorporated that type of exercise into our home reading. By not explaining "the why," the school missed an opportunity to engage me as a partner, and to help me learn a new skill for working with my child.

Many schools have security systems, right? Buzzers, computerized sign-in programs, badges. All of these things can be a little off-putting to families. But if we take the time to explain *why* we have all of this security in place, parents will be okay with it. So explain: "Please check in so we can welcome you and help keep your child safe." Or "Our doorbell is just like your doorbell; it gives us a chance to properly welcome you." Who wouldn't want to be welcomed, and who wouldn't want to make sure their child was safe?

Explaining why can also mean explaining the big picture. If I'm a parent and I'm engaged by you to help with something, please let me know what I will get out of it, or let me know what my student will get out of it. Explain to me what fluency is, and why it will help my child become a stronger reader. Let me know the bigger goal we're working toward so that I can truly feel like I'm a part of it. I might even have some ideas to contribute.

Do Include an "Ask"

So often we give parents information . . . and that's that. We don't always go the extra mile by including an "ask." And parents are left thinking, *It's great to know and understand the new standards, but what do you want me to do?*

There's probably an ask in all of our communications with parents. Sometimes it's unspoken: "I'm asking you to stay in touch." Sometimes it's spoken: "The one thing you can do this year is check the red folder. Is that doable?" In my opinion, all of our "asks" should be clear and spelled out.

The key to our "asks" is to offer up what we will do first. "If you call or email me, I will get back to you by the end of the day. Can you make sure I have the best number to reach you?" All relationships and partnerships are built on give and take, and creating strong relationships and partnerships with our parents happens the same way.

Here's an example. We wrote a letter to send home to parents whose children did not pass the state's standardized reading test. We included what we would do, and we included an "ask" of parents.

> *We want to do everything possible to make sure your child passes, but we will need your help. We need you to sign your child up for our summer reading program.*

We went on to include details on the program, and we made a point to say we were providing bus transportation. And finally, we thanked our parents for their partnership and support.

With many things in life, people want to help, they want to support the work; sometimes they are just waiting to be asked, and our parents are no different.

Do Include "The How"

Making an ask is important, but it is also sometimes important to include "the how." Many times, when we ask parents to help with projects or assignments, we assume they know how to help. Sometimes they don't know how to help, and they can end up feeling lost, or worse yet, not capable of helping.

I once ran a focus group of grandparents raising their grandchildren. The first topic they brought up was homework. They told me they were frustrated. Their children were all in elementary school and, each night, they would bring home math problems with all kinds of boxes, lines, and dashes. The grandparents said they knew how to do math, but they did not know how to help their children work the problems using boxes, lines, and dashes.

This particular group was made up of grandparents, but many younger parents and caregivers feel this way, too. I can remember when my kids were in elementary school; I also struggled to figure out the boxes, lines, and dashes. And I did feel overwhelmed. But even worse, I felt a little embarrassed in front of my children. I was ashamed that I didn't know how to help them.

This focus group of grandparents was on fire that night, and came up with a couple of great solutions. They suggested that teachers send home simple "parent" instructions to go along with the homework. They also suggested teachers post short videos on social media to show how to do the problems.

Bottom line is, if we hope parents will partner with us and help their children at home, we've got to provide them with the skills, training, and materials they need.

Do Use Relatable Examples

In many instances, we can use what might be considered common knowledge and experiences to help us convey our messages.

So when we're trying to explain DIBELS, we can say, "It's like when you go to the doctor's office and they take your blood pressure and weight. Those are just quick ways to measure your health. DIBELS is a quick way to check in and measure your child's reading skills." In this example, we assume parents have visited the doctor, but again, it's always nice to convey the message in another way, just in case they haven't.

Use this technique carefully, always being aware that your cultural experiences may differ from your families' experiences. For example, you may not want to say, "You know, like when you go to a beach in Florida," because the family you're talking with may never have visited Florida, or even traveled at all. Using an example like this may make a parent feel more like an outsider, disengaged, and closed off from you or the rest of your parents.

Do Rock the "Rule of Three"

We like things presented in threes. For some reason, audiences and readers are more likely to remember information when it's delivered in three parts. Think, "Life, Liberty, and the Pursuit of Happiness." Or "Blood, Sweat, and Tears." Or even, "Stop, Drop, and Roll." See, I just did it!

Not only are audiences and readers more likely to remember information in threes, they find it more interesting, more persuasive, and more enjoyable. The "Rule of Three" creates a pattern. So if you need to share information with parents, try to present it in a way that makes the most of the Rule of Three. If you have more than three ideas to present or talk about, try to divide those up into a beginning, middle, and end.

Back in the day, whenever I did live reports, I used the Rule of Three. I'd think, *what are the three most important ideas, facts, or points,* and then I tried to organize my live shots using an introduction, those three points, and a conclusion. I didn't try to cram a ton of information into my live presentations. I just tried to keep it simple.

One way to think about this is to go back to the thoughts you had about the goal and purpose of your conversation. What exactly do your parents need to know? Or what do you want them to know about something? Concentrate on that. Then fill in just a few details. For example, it's not important that our parents know the way we organize our tutoring program. It is important for them to know what the program is and why it will benefit their child, when and where it meets, and how to sign up.

Another way to look at it is to ask yourself what you want them to remember or take away from your conversation, article, or letter. Then think, *I want them to remember three things,* at which point you conclude what those three most important things are and communicate them. What you don't want to do is give them five takeaways and hope they remember the most important ones. The Rule of Three will help you keep the information you share digestible. Now that I've pointed out the Rule of Three, you'll start noticing it in the book. Sorry about that.

Do Cull the Herd!

This same advice to pare down information also applies to the activities and learning-at-home resources you recommend to parents.

A few years ago, I was working with a school that sent a weekly email to parents. Within that email, the school included 15 links to websites parents could check out for more resources and activities they could use to help their children improve their reading. Fifteen links! What parent has the time to open that many web pages? Go ahead and "cull the herd!" Make it easy on your parents by doing the work for them. Here's where you *can* flex your authority and expertise; you decide which sites are best and most helpful and understandable for your parents. And then give them a choice of no more than three. They'll feel less overwhelmed and more likely to use the resources and do the activities that you've provided.

THE DON'TS

Now that you have a good handle on what *to do,* it's time to take a look at what *not* to do. These "don'ts" are just as important . . . maybe even more so. Because they can easily create an information barrier, or worse, leave parents feeling disconnected and disengaged.

Don't Assume Knowledge

In Chapter 2, I talk about working with the academic team to translate assessments for parents into explanations they could understand. Well, at one point, I pointed out to one of the members of the assessment team that the word "differentiation" was not a word that parents would understand. And she said, "They should." *Whoa . . . I hardly knew where to go with that!* First off, "should" sounds awfully judgmental and that's not very partner-y. And second, it assumes knowledge.

When it comes to communicating with our parents, we cannot assume that they bring knowledge and understanding of our rules, language, or processes to the table. Such assumptions can be off-putting and alienating to parents, but most of all, when you assume knowledge, you risk losing your audience. It's like coming into a conversation midstream. Parents will spend the whole time (or conversation) reading your letter and trying to figure out what you're talking about. They will either quit listening or reading, or they'll miss whatever information you're relaying to them. Even if they get the information, they will have no context for it. Or they may feel talked down to, intimidated, or excluded.

I'm sure this has happened to you before. Think about a time when you got to a meeting late and had to try to figure out what was going on. It's that same feeling.

Pretty uncomfortable.

In my broadcast writing class one year, I had a student who was not your typical college student. He was, is, an oncologist. He took the class just to learn more about news, but he told me recently that his whole approach with his patients changed as a result of taking the class. He is now acutely aware of the medical jargon he uses and goes to great effort to make sure he is communicating on a level that his patients understand.

But more than that, he doesn't assume that his patients understand stuff. He's not in the "they-should-know" mode. He even gave me a great example. Sometimes he has to tell his patients news like, "the median survival rate for this type of cancer is six months." He will stop and explain what "median" means, just to make sure they understand. He knows that if he doesn't, odds are the patient will hear, 'I've got six months to live." And that's not the case. What it actually means is that after six months, half of all people will still be alive. You can imagine, when it comes to important information on things like survival, clear communication is incredibly important.

My doctor-student doesn't assume that patients bring any knowledge to the appointment, but he does acknowledge that they are the experts when it comes to their bodies. His approach is respectful, and as you can imagine, patients love him.

So if I don't assume knowledge, how much background information do I need to give parents?

Good question.

Keep in mind, you're trying to convey information in short, understandable ways. So again, your background information doesn't have to start at the very beginning. (I often joke and say, "It doesn't have to start way back to when Adam met Eve.") It's enough to say or write, "You may recall last year that the state approved a new standardized test." That statement alone does several things. It helps parents remember, if they have forgotten, and it helps put into context the new information that you're about to share. Plus, it's positive. It's assuming that your parents are aware ("you may recall") and that they care, while at the same time, it's respectfully giving them the necessary background information if they *aren't* aware. It also prepares them to hear what you're going to say next.

Think about this example from the world of education. Many of our parents may not have graduated from high school or gone to college. So you can't start talking about the SAT and assume they understand what it's all about. And even if they did go to college, many of the processes around college applications have completely changed. When I went to school, there was no "standard" college application. I knew nothing about that when my kids got to high school and started thinking about college applications. So assuming that even your more experienced parents bring knowledge to the table can be a mistake.

So in the course of a conversation about college applications, first take the time to define standardized tests and standardized applications, and then move the conversation on to the rest of the information.

We can assume that most parents understand basic things about school and about the school day. Most people have this frame of reference. But anything beyond that . . . well, you're taking your chances. After all, the schools of today often do not look like the schools of yesterday.

Don't Get Lost in the Details

This may be a hard one for you. But it isn't necessary to include every detail when you're talking or writing to a parent.

Keep thinking about those three tiers of information. If you're still struggling, try thinking of it this way: It's like writing for television versus newspaper or online communications. When you write for TV news, the point is to give viewers the basics, just what they need to know. If they want to know more, they can pick up a newspaper or jump online to read more.

Try to take the same approach in your communications with parents. Include only the details that are important for your parents to know and understand.

Here are some examples: It's okay to say "the state" instead of the "Montana Department of Education." It's okay to say "state law" instead of "Public Law 109." In the first instance, parents don't need the official name of the Department of Education to understand what you're trying to communicate. And in the second example, they don't need to know the actual number of the law. It doesn't aid in their understanding of the law.

It's also okay to just write, as I do in this book, "research shows," without the actual name of the researcher and date of the research.

If you're using simple words and sticking to one thought per sentence, you'll probably naturally leave out unnecessary details.

Here is a great example from a letter that is sent to the parents of third graders in Indiana. The letter is designed to let them know about a new standardized test.

It also includes a few parent tips.

> *As you may know, in March of 2010, the Indiana General Assembly passed House Enrolled Act 1367 (also known as Public Law 108 in 2010) requiring the evaluation of reading skills for all third grade students.*

Honestly, parents don't need to know *any* of these details. It is simply not necessary that they know the name of the law. It does not help them in their understanding, and frankly, it's just clutter. It also leaves you wondering what *is* important in this sentence?

We can easily condense and simplify this:

> *Each year, the state of Indiana requires that we test all third graders to see how well they are reading and understanding what they read.*

Much shorter, much clearer, much cleaner, and easier to understand.

The key is to make sure the words you're using and the message you're conveying are still accurate.

Again, tell parents what they need to know, but in the interest of their time and attention span, spare them all the details.

Don't Assume They Get It

Just as you can't assume knowledge, you also can't assume that if you've told a parent something once, or sent home a letter about it, that the parent understands what you're trying to tell them. You can't think, *I made an automated phone call about the PTA meeting, so I've communicated and can cross that off my to-do list.*

Research shows that people don't grasp information until they're ready to hear it. Think about it. You can send someone the directions to your house a week before your party, but chances are they will not read them and map out a route until it's time to go.

You can start talking to me about college and a career for my kid when he's in middle school, but I may not retain or grasp the information until I need to know it. However, that can change if you communicate to me *why* I need to know it when my kid is in the sixth grade. If you make a good case, I will pay attention, but you still might have to tell me more than once.

Research shows that people have to be exposed to new ideas at least three times in order to remember and understand them. When we write stories in broadcasting, we have this little saying, "Tell them what you are going to tell them, tell them, and then tell them what you just told them."

In other words, prepare people for what you're going to tell them, tell them, and then give it your best chance at being understood by telling them again.

Don't Assume They'll Tell You If They Don't Get It

If I were in front of you now, I would ask you to raise your hand if you've ever sat through a meeting or a professional development program where you didn't understand something. If so, did you speak out and say so? Probably not. And if not, why didn't you?

I'll take a guess that you were embarrassed, fearful of looking clueless, or just too intimidated; maybe you figured that if you continued to listen, you'd eventually catch on. It happens to all of us. Maybe for you it happens when you talk to your mechanic, maybe it happens when you meet with your doctor. It's a horrible feeling. But even though it feels bad, and we tell ourselves there are no "stupid" questions, we usually don't want to put ourselves out there.

Families don't either. Most will not admit they don't understand something. So it's up to us to constantly check in with them and make sure they do understand.

In one-on-one encounters, people are more likely to ask questions or tell you they don't understand something. So after a presentation or conversation, you may want to pull a few parents aside and check to see if they understood you. Maybe you can check in with the parents who are the last to leave or those who come up to chat afterward. You could also follow up with a phone call and ask. But try not to say, "Do you have any questions?" That approach can be a bit off-putting. Parents may feel like they should have questions, or like they're not smart if they don't. Instead, take a softer approach, "I'm not sure I did a good job explaining that . . . did it all make sense?" or "Are we good?" A softer approach can open the door for communication.

ENGAGE YOUR AUDIENCE

After you've run through your "Dos" and "Don'ts," focused on the content of your message, and tailored it to your parents, it's time to think more deeply about

how the information will be processed and how it will be received. And again, this
starts with you putting yourself in your parents' shoes, heads, and hearts.

Warm Things Up

In the rush of life, we sometimes forget how important it is to stop and greet
one another, either in person or by email or text. Instead, we get right to the point
with our message or our conversation.

But these little niceties that we exchange, the quick "I hope you had a good
weekend," or "I hope you're safe and well," really matter. They help us build
relationships. We do want to streamline our communications, but in the decision
about what to include and what to leave out, a warm greeting—that cheery
"Hello"—is essential.

What Emotional Place Are Your Parents Coming from?

Think for a moment about the passion you feel for your family. And then think
about the passion our parents have for their children. They can't turn their passion
and love off; it's at the very core of every interaction between you and your families.

Perhaps you've had parents raise their voices at you, cry in front of you, or
hug you. These are all ways they show their passion and love for their kids. They're
concerned, and they worry about their children. If you can keep that in mind, and
acknowledge it when you interact with your parents, it will help you build a bridge
with them.

I made a presentation to a group of school secretaries once in which they
talked about how parents sometimes come into the school angry, even belligerent.
I first acknowledged how difficult that must be for them, and then I suggested
that they look at those angry parents in a different way. Those upset moms and
dads were actually super-engaged in advocating and fighting for their children.
There was complete silence. It was quite a moment! It doesn't necessarily make
dealing with angry parents any easier for those secretaries, but viewing the parents'
anger as a positive might help them keep their cool and not take the parents' anger
personally.

Here's yet another example. I was once asked to work on a short explanation
of school safety procedures. The document was very official and, in my opinion,
somewhat cold. As I thought about it and talked about it with someone I worked
with (which is always helpful), I came to the conclusion that what was missing was

simply the acknowledgement of the love and concern that parents have for their children. Instead of writing, "In the event of a lockdown, do not come to school to get your child," it is much more respectful to acknowledge the terror a parent would feel in the event of a lockdown. So if we write, "We know your first thought is to come to school to get your child, but it is safer to wait until the lockdown is over," this acknowledges and is respectful of parents' feelings. By writing something a little softer (and by including "the why"—"it is safer"), we seem less like we're ordering parents around, less like we know best, and more like we're partners in protecting their children.

Here's another example, and again, it involves school safety. This time I was working on a letter to parents about new safety procedures at a school. The idea of an intruder in a school is scary stuff for parents, and for many reasons, most of them don't want to talk about this scary stuff with their children. But we, as school personnel, have to. So I acknowledged that from the start by writing something like, "We realize that thinking about safety and safety scenarios can be difficult. We will take great care to be reassuring with students and help them develop confidence by knowing what to do in an emergency."

This statement reassures parents that we understand the delicate nature of this subject and that we will be very aware of it and protective when we talk and work with their children. The statement also has a "parenting" feel; that is, we will be reassuring, which is what parents often do with their children. It's very partnership-like, rather than authoritative or just informative, because it acknowledges parents' emotions.

Here's my last example.

I was once pulled into a meeting with one of our school's community partners. The partnering agency was working with our school district on a program for children who were dealing with mental health issues. Agency staff had written a brochure for parents of students in the program. The brochure began something like this:

The Student Day Treatment Program is a psychiatric partial hospitalization program for children Kindergarten through 6th grade who are diagnosed as having a serious emotional disorder.

Believe me, the rest of it didn't get any more uplifting. I read it over and asked two questions:

> *"When do you hand this out to parents?"*
> *One of the staff members replied, "When we're enrolling children in the program."*

> *"And where are those parents emotionally?" I asked.*
> *"Great point. We never really thought about that."*

The agency handed the brochures out to parents right after they told those parents their children needed to attend the day treatment program. In other words, they were handed out right after those parents were told their students needed more than a traditional school setting could provide.

Think about it. That's scary and upsetting enough, but when coupled with "psychiatric partial hospitalization" . . . well, you get the picture.

In this situation, it was so important to convey a sense of comfort to these parents, that we rewrote the brochure and when we finished, it felt like a hug. The message, wording, and tone all worked together to convey the idea that the program was a special place designed to help both students and parents succeed.

When You Share, Make 'Em Care

I had a journalism professor whose voice still echoes in my head: "Make me care . . . make me care." Her idea was that in the bombardment of messages and communications out there, it's the ones that make you care, that touch you emotionally, that get through to people.

"Make me care" can be hard to explain. It builds on all of the ideas I've shared, including that parents have strong emotions for their children and that, if we explain "the why," we can engage parents more effectively. It also builds on how well you know your audience.

What it comes down to is the understanding that if you really think about who your parents are, what they are like, what they know, how busy they are, what they like to do, and so on, you can come up with an angle that will make them perk up and pay attention.

For example, in the news media, if we say to you, "Your taxes are going up this year," guess what? You care! In education, if we say to parents, "If your child misses even one day a month, he may not graduate on time," guess what? They care!

Making parents care is really about including one or two facts or details that will resonate or touch them in an emotional way and help them pay attention to your information. Think about it this way: it's kinda like hitting them in the heart. Here's a positive example. Say that you call a parent and you begin by saying, "Your child is amazing." Guess what? Now that parent cares. That parent is actively listening and waiting for what you will say next.

The "make-me-care" angle can also be sharing facts that you think parents will find interesting. Don't just tell them that a career fair will take place at the high school. Instead, let them know that six companies will be there hiring summer workers and that every student will be offered a job. Don't just let them know a reading fair is coming up; let them know what's happening there that will be worth their time—like, "You will have a chance to speak with your child's teacher, you can sign up for a library card, and you will leave with one simple idea that you can use when you read to your child." Those kinds of facts will make parents care.

Remember, parents may have a dozen things on their minds, have a million places to go, or a million things to do. We've already talked about how you can't and shouldn't include every fact and detail, so you need to think, *What bit of information can I include that will help ensure that I am heard?*

Sometimes you can accomplish the "make-me-care" effect just by showing that *you* care. If you're willing to put in the time and effort to have conversations and build relationships with your parents, they may be more likely to pay attention to what you have to say. They may think, *I know her and trust her, and if she has something to say, I'm going to listen. If she cares that much, I will too.*

Remember, as an educator, you have the ability to inspire not only the students you work with, but also their parents. That's a privilege.

Gracias, Merci, Thank You

Often we forget to thank parents.

It's nice to end all your conversations and communications with something similar to "Thank you for all you do to help your child succeed." Or "Thank you so much for taking the time to come in and meet with me." It's respectful, partner-like, and warm.

TYING IT ALL TOGETHER

Here's a "before" and "after" example that ties it all together. This is part of a newsletter article from a middle school I worked with a couple of years ago. The audience for the article is parents and caregivers. Many of those parents and caregivers work full-time (sometimes more than one job). Some did not graduate from high school. And some are grandparents raising grandkids. Stop for a second, take off your "educator hat" and put on your "parent/caregiver hat." Now read this over and think about the information included. What information is important to these busy families? What information is necessary for them to know and what information could be left out? Where do we assume knowledge? How are we taking into account the emotional connection? Did we include "the why"? And what information is missing? As you read this over, you'll probably recognize that this newsletter article is written in a very formal style with *lots* of five-dollar words.

> *Our ELA students are taking their second Reading Inventory (RI) assessment for this school year. According to the National Center of Intensive Interventions, the RI is "a research-based, computer-adaptive reading assessment for students in grades K–12 that measures reading comprehension on the Lexile Framework for Reading. The student is asked to read a passage taken from an authentic text and then choose the option that best fills the blank in the last statement. To complete the statement, the student must respond on a literal level (recall a fact) or inferential level (determine the main idea of the passage, draw an inference from the material presented, or make a connection between sentences in the passage)." Their scores reveal if they are below basic, basic, proficient, or advanced readers. In 7th grade, a student is proficient with a score range of 925 to 1100. An 8th grader is proficient with a score range of 970 – 1150. You will receive your student's current Lexile level in their Qtr. 2 report card envelopes. Until then, please ask your student about his/her score. We are truly excited and encouraged about the growth shown on our students' second reading assessment; they will take their last RI during 4th quarter.*

When we stop and think about our parents, we can quickly see that half of the information in this article . . . the National Center for Intensive Interventions, computer adaptive, literal level, inferential level, etc., could all be left out. It's all

Tier 2 or maybe even Tier 3 information. Sure, there may be parents interested in that level of detail, but we're trying to reach all parents with our newsletter, and create a broad understanding. The information combined with the formal writing and five-dollar words (that we assume parents understand) make this article difficult to read.

Here's a rewrite of the article. Notice the information we included, the information we left out, and the information we added. While you're reading, notice the conversational style elements.

> *Happy Holidays 7th and 8th Grade Parents and Students!*
>
> *Your students have been busy this past month seeing how much they've improved their Reading! They've taken a test called the Reading Inventory or RI. RI is designed to test how well students understand or comprehend what they read.*
>
> *With RI, your student reads something on a computer and then answers questions. Those answers help us see where your student is with reading compared to where they need to be for the year.*
>
> *There are four levels in RI: below basic, basic, proficient and advanced. Your student's level depends on their score. These scores are called Lexile Levels. When we know your student's Lexile Level, we can better tailor our teaching and help them become a stronger reader.*
>
> *You will be getting your child's Lexile score in the next report card. We will provide a key for you to understand the score. Please look over your child's score and ask your child about their Lexile level. We will also send home suggestions on how you can help your child become a stronger reader. Until then, please reach out if you'd like tips, or if you have any questions.*

Still not perfect, perhaps a bit long, but it captures the essential information, does not assume knowledge, explains "the why," makes an "ask," includes emotion, and is much, much easier to read. It's classic Tier 1: basic information presented in a clear, concise way that allows all parents to take part in the learning process.

"Communi-Create"

Keep in mind, you'll have better luck at making sure your information is received and processed if you share it in a variety of ways, so be creative.

Offer your information one-on-one, in written form, through video communications (helpful for visual learners and parents challenged at reading), by phone and so on. Repeated exposure through different sources will help ensure that your audience (your families) has heard and understood your information. Remember, if you tell them some information face to face, they might be preoccupied. If you send home a letter with the same information, they might glance at it, but not fully grasp it. But if you also post the information on social media, you'll probably make the connection you need to. Reaching out from all sides helps cut through the clutter of life.

Better yet, survey parents at the beginning of the year and ask them: "What's the best way we can communicate this year?" Or "What is the best way to reach you?" Tailoring your communications to your parents, just as you tailor instruction, can help you make sure that your information is received.

Keep in mind, it's great to present information in clear, concise ways, using understandable language, but our ultimate goal is to build relationships that allow us to forge partnerships. Our words and information open the door by giving parents the knowledge they need to participate in the real work—the work of truly sharing in and advocating for their children's education.

The Nuances of Tone and Body Language

It isn't enough to deliver "just the facts" in a way that parents and caregivers can understand; as I've said, it's important to deliver your message in a way that expresses a partnership approach. So once you understand the basics of good conversational style and know what you want to say, you can begin thinking about your tone of voice and the body language you're displaying.

Researchers have found that non-verbal communication makes up between 65 and 85 percent of communication, depending on the context. In many cases, the old adage is true . . . it's less about what you say and more about how you say it.

TONE

So what exactly is tone? It's the attitude or emotion you express toward the subject, the listener, or the reader through your choice of words and phrases. No matter what you say, your written or verbal tone of voice determines how what you say will be received and understood. In other words, tone starts with your emotion, but also brings out an emotion in the person that you are communicating with.

When it comes to our tone, we're often unaware of the attitudes and moods that we bring into our conversations, emails, and notes. If we haven't checked our assumptions about our parents, or taken time to reflect on *our* mood that day, our tone may come across as less than friendly, and not express the patience, respect, or understanding that we need to build relationships.

Just take a minute to think about your own life. How many times have you answered your phone when you were right in the middle of something? Think about how you probably came across: anxious, rushed, maybe even annoyed. What message did that send to the person calling? That person didn't know you were in the middle of something. All they knew, all they could *sense,* was that you weren't very warm and friendly. Unless you make it a point to say, "I'm so sorry. I know I'm coming across a little rushed; I was right in the middle of something," you can leave your caller with a negative impression.

Here's another example. When my children were younger, I was a stay-at-home mom. One day, my husband came home from work and asked, "So, what did you do today?" Except he didn't just ask, "So, what did you do today?" He asked, "So, what did you *do* today?" Just that little stressing of the word "do" set me off. It came across as very judgmental, as though I were sitting around eating bonbons. He absolutely did not mean anything by it. It was more about me and the way I felt about staying home. It played on my feelings and my sense of self-worth, and I found myself feeling defensive. His words evoked an unintended emotional response.

Just as you and I do, our students' parents bring feelings about their self-worth and their confidence into their parenting. And when we adjust our tone, even with only one word, we can come across as judgmental, doubtful, or know-it-alls.

Let's be honest. People respond more to tone than words, which means that tone can be everything. The fact of it is, we may think we can always recognize when we're stressed out or angry, but we can't, and this stress and anger can creep into our communications with families.

STRIKING A PARTNERSHIP TONE

The first step to improving your tone is to realize it starts with you. As we talked about, it's important to spend some time thinking about the families you are communicating with, and remembering that they want the best for their children. If you do that, you'll be well on your way to striking the caring, warm tone of a partner.

Take Stock of Your Emotions

We all know schools can be fast-paced, stressful places. We have a lot to do in a short amount of time. Pressure to show success on tests is mounting. Each of our students has a different personality, and we are constantly trying to adjust. There are multiple demands for our time, and on top of that, we do have personal lives (remember those?), and sometimes what's happening at home bleeds into how we interact at work.

We're often unaware of these realities. So before we interact with parents or caregivers, it's important for us to pause and think about where we are with our own emotions. Are we stressed or upset? Did that last conversation with the principal get to us? Did we sleep okay last night? Are we hungry? All of these things can affect how we come across to others. Are we making a positive phone call to a parent because we were told to, or because we want to? Do we feel rushed? Pausing to reflect before we speak is crucial to our success in communicating and reaching out to families. Remember, they don't know any of this is going on. All they know is how we're coming across to them.

Take Stock of Your Negative Attitudes

Whether we know it or not, we all bring our life experiences to every conversation we have. Maybe we've had negative experiences with some families in the past. Maybe we've had negative experiences with just one type of parent, maybe it's someone who isn't like us, someone we're not entirely comfortable with. Maybe it was our fault, maybe it wasn't. Either way, we need to stop and think about the prior experiences that we may be bringing to the table.

Just by our tone, our negative experiences can come across as condescending, insincere, or worst of all, judgmental. We may talk with parents about their child's reading level, but if we don't believe they can truly understand, those parents will sense it. When this happens, the conversations become less about an equal exchange of ideas or imparting of important information and more about obligation. That can actually hurt our relationships with our parents.

As I said previously, just as we bring our experiences to the conversations and interactions we have with families, they bring theirs. They are filtering what we say through their own experiences and frame of reference trying, like we are, to fit what we're saying or writing into their experiences. If they've spent years believing that school is scary, we, as educators, will also be scary. That's why we need to check our attitudes and assumptions at the door, and start from as neutral a place as possible.

How do you do this? You can start by being aware of the fact that your attitudes about people do affect your communications. It's impossible not to bring your attitudes or assumptions to a conversation; after all, in many cases, these assumptions help us organize information and make sense of the world. But be aware of these assumptions and of what they are so that you can begin to look at every conversation or email as a clean slate.

Remember, even if you've had a negative experience with a parent or caregiver, perhaps that person was having a bad or stressed day. Give that person a fresh start, too. Try not to generalize. Everyone is different, and everyone deserves honest, true dialogue.

What's My Goal, Again?

Is your goal to build a relationship? Get action? Explain something? Knowing why you're communicating in the first place can help you set the tone for the interaction.

If, for example, you're calling a parent with good news, you may want to have a cheerful, celebratory, lighthearted tone. If, on the other hand, you have some not-so-good information, you may want to spend time thinking about the proper tone for the conversation. Because the parent may be upset by the news, going into the conversation with an understanding attitude and using softer words and reassuring tones might help ease the conversation. You might choose words and tones that are less direct, defensive, and authoritative.

In both communications, it's important to convey a sense of partnership.

And remember, in any conversation or any communication, no matter how challenging, your goal is not to "win" or "be right." It's to forge a relationship with a parent that helps a student succeed. If you keep this in mind, it will help you maintain the right tone and help you "keep your cool."

Remove Your Teacher Hat

As educators, we use several styles of communication every day.

We have discussions in which we talk through the pros and cons of a situation, maybe with ourselves, maybe with our students. We lead and spark debates where we try to persuade others, or help students persuade each other.

But we often spend the majority of our teaching day saying things like, "Your homework is due tomorrow," "Remember, we walk on the right side of the hallway," and "Here's the formula for this equation." In other words, we're "in charge." Even if you see yourself as more of a "coach" in the learning process, you still have a goal at the end of the lesson. You know where you want your students to go, and where you want them to be at the end of the lesson, activity, or conversation.

It's easy to see how sometimes this "teacher" style of communicating, this authoritative tone, can slip into our conversations and communications with families.

The only truly symmetrical, or equal, form of communicating is dialogue where there is a true exchange of ideas. Dialogue requires both talking and listening. Think of it as two peers or two equal partners collaborating on a project to discover a shared understanding. A true dialogue conveys the message that each person's ideas and views are essential.

This is where we want to be with our parents and caregivers, where there's an openness and a spirit of cooperation. We can convey that with our tone by speaking slower, softer, and with less force. We can convey that with our words by:

> Acknowledging the parent as the expert: *"I know you know him best."*
> Asking questions: *"How have you handled this?"*
> Using "we" and "our": *"I'm excited we can work together on this! Our work is paying off!"*

But above all, listen. And respond in a way that shows you listened. Incorporate parental concerns and suggestions, and celebrate successes together.

Be Friendly, Especially When You're Not Feeling It!

Every day we are bombarded by conversations and, in many instances, we listen only halfheartedly. But think about it, we are more likely to relax, pay attention, and participate in conversations when we are greeted or received with a friendly voice.

Even if we don't feel friendly, we can cultivate a friendly voice. Here's how:

> *Think about what a friendly voice sounds like.*
> *Practice speaking in a friendly voice.*
> *Change up word emphasis.*

Smile while you speak.
Think about friendly people.
Speak slowly and calmly.

It's my experience that even when I'm in a lousy mood (it happens most often when I'm shopping for groceries in our large supercenter), if I greet other shoppers or the checkout people in a friendly voice, I feel friendly. Being friendly has a way of changing my mood.

BODY LANGUAGE

Communicating involves so many layers that sometimes the importance of body language can be overlooked. But research shows that body language accounts for 50 to 70 percent of all communication.

Body language consists of the nonverbal signals we send through our facial expressions, body movements, and the position of our eyes and eye movements. Often we may be saying one thing, but our body language is saying another. So as you strive to interact on a respectful level with parents, it's important to be aware of your body language.

It's also important to be aware of some of the cultural differences when it comes to body language. For example, in some cultures, gesturing with the thumb and forefinger today means "okay." In other cultures, it's seen as vulgar. As you're working to become a stronger communicator, take some time to learn about the cultures of the families in your school.

Take a Breath

Friendly, open body language starts with the breath. If you are relaxed, you will look relaxed. So before you sit down to meet with parents, or before you hit the "camera on" button for your virtual parent conference, take a few deep breaths. You can do this by placing one hand on your chest and one on your stomach. When you breathe, try not to move your upper hand . . . in other words, take deep breaths using your diaphragm. After three to five slow breaths, you'll start to feel your shoulders sink a little lower and you'll feel your facial muscles relax.

Your Face

If you're relaxed, your face will show it. Likewise, if you're angry or upset, it will show on your face. When you're greeting parents, start by smiling. And make sure your smile feels and looks sincere. Otherwise, it could come across as fake.

When you're not smiling, relax your tongue and your lips. Try to avoid covering your mouth. This can come across as you being closed off, or it can imply you are uncomfortable or even hiding something. And try not to turn down your lips. A parent might interpret this as anger, disapproval, or insincerity.

Make sure your cheeks are relaxed. You may want to slightly raise your eyebrows just a little bit. This will indicate interest. And if it's culturally appropriate, make eye contact. This will also indicate interest. If you're looking around, you may make a parent feel you're bored, uninterested, or uncomfortable. But do break your gaze from time to time. If you're "staring" at your parents or caregivers, you may come across as threatening.

Whether you're in a virtual or in-person conversation, go ahead and nod from time to time. Nodding can be a subtle way of indicating you're listening. If you agree with what your parents are saying, you may also want to add some verbal reinforcement to your nod: "I completely agree," or "You are so right." All of this can make a parent feel heard.

Finally (and I find this one hard to remember), try tilting your head to one side during conversations. This can also indicate interest and shows that you're open and listening and really thinking about what's being said. These are all subtle ways your face can help you build the trust you need to engage parents.

That Conversation Your Body's Having

When you talk on the phone, or send an email, you don't have an opportunity to use body language to enhance your communications with parents. But in face-to-face conversations and when you are communicating virtually, you do. You can use your body language to soften an interaction and forge a closer relationship.

In order to come across as open and friendly, stand in a relaxed way, with your shoulders down and back and your arms relaxed and open. If your arms are crossed, you could be sending a message that you're closed off or unreachable. Or worse yet, anxious, scared, or exasperated. If your hands are on your hips, this can appear to some as an intimidating stance.

If you're standing, try to maintain a socially acceptable distance apart from parents. No close talkers! Anything closer can make parents uncomfortable. But keep in mind, sometimes there's a large cultural component to physical space that you'll want to be aware of if you are working with families from different backgrounds. In some cultures, it's the norm to stand much closer to people than we do in the United States.

If you're sitting, lean forward a little. This will show you're engaged and listening; if you're sitting and leaning back, you may convey that you're distant and unapproachable, or even arrogant.

In order to come across as friendly and open, it's important to keep your hands in view and your palms relaxed and open. If you're fidgeting with something like a paperclip on your desk (and I do this *all* the time), you run the risk of coming across as bored, nervous, or upset. If you're like me, keep your fidgeting to a minimum. And remember to put your phone away so you're not temped to fidget with it. This will also help the parent see that they have your undivided attention.

Send Positive Nonverbal Messages

It's not just your mood, the information you have to deliver, or your body language that can affect the tone of your communications. It can also be your surroundings.

Sitting behind a big desk can make you feel authoritative, but might make parents feel like they aren't partners. Getting up, sitting next to parents, and talking in a comfortable setting are all things that can help you ease the tone of the conversations and influence how the communications are received.

Consider meeting parents at the front door, just as you would if they were visiting your home. Make chitchat as you walk them to your classroom, or better yet, take them to the most comfortable room in the school, preferably one with nice comfy chairs. Make sure you're sitting at the same level and in the same type of chair. If you have to meet in a classroom, join them in the student desks. And if possible, sit to one side. This will convey the message that you view your parents as equals. As a parent, there's nothing worse than having to cram yourself into a grade-school-sized chair to speak with a teacher who's standing up or even sitting on a desk; you immediately feel like a child (a cramped and uncomfortable child), and not an equal partner.

Think about whether you really need papers for the discussion. If so, try not to write information down during the conversation. This can be really intimidating; some parents will wonder what you're writing and perhaps even feel judged. If you have to, ask permission: "Do you mind if I write some of this down so I don't forget?" And always, no matter what, make sure your conversation takes place in a private area.

I was once waiting in a school lobby for a conversation with a principal. A little boy was sitting in the chair next to me. He had his knees pulled up to his chest, and his feet were on the chair's seat; it was almost as though he were rolled into a little ball. A man, the boy's father, came into the lobby. You could sense the tension. He spoke to the secretary, and then an administrator came out of an office and immediately proceeded to tell the father everything that the student had done wrong that day, right there in the lobby!

At first, I ignored the conversation and tried to fiddle with my phone. Finally, in a very loud voice, I asked the secretary if there was somewhere else I could wait because I wanted to give the family some privacy. I didn't see the end of the conversation, but my heart broke for both the father and the student.

Looking back, there is no doubt it had been "one of those days." The administrator was busy, and she didn't mean to approach the conversation that way, out in the open. But even on "one of those days," it's important to remember to be thoughtful.

The Power of Coffee (or Water)

So, imagine for a second . . .

What if that father walked in and the school administrator not only greeted him warmly and escorted him to a private room, but offered him a cup of coffee or a glass of water. Just imagine for a second how that simple gesture could have changed the dynamic of the interaction.

When parents come to our school, or join us in a virtual setting, they are our partners, but they are also our guests. We are asking them to enter our space. And it's important to show them a bit of hospitality.

Offering a cup of coffee isn't just welcoming, it's a way of communicating. It says, "I'm going to spend some time with you . . . at least as much time as it takes for you to drink a cup of coffee . . . and we are going to sit down together and get this figured out." It conveys partnership, care, and respect. It's a simple gesture that packs a lot of power and is so easy to do.

VIRTUALLY SPEAKING

When you're communicating with parents virtually, whether you're using Facetime or Skype or Zoom or another app, you'll want to keep in mind all of the body language tips from earlier . . . use hand gestures, smile and nod, etc. But there are some additional things to think about.

Chat 'Em Up

In my reporter days, I used to interview people who would see the camera and get nervous. I knew if they were nervous, I would not get a good "sound bite," or snippet, that I could use for my story. So I had a strategy for helping them relax. I would chitchat with them while we were setting up the camera, and continue the chitchat even after we started recording the interview. The banter seemed to help them get out some of their nerves and help them relax into the interview. Take the same approach when it comes to your virtual conversations. Once you start the meeting, before you get to the purpose of the conversation, spend some time discussing the weather or the holidays, or whatever. Try to avoid asking parents what they do, or where they work, as this might make them uncomfortable. You don't want to make them feel self-conscious, or worse, like you might be judging them. Instead, try asking questions like, "How has your day been going?" or "Before we really get started, I'd love to hear your favorite thing about your child."

Chitchat will help take away some of the awkwardness of talking into a camera and it will ensure that everyone on the virtual chat is relaxed and comfortable (including you!).

Tech Barriers

After the chitchat, it's always nice to acknowledge the barriers of virtual communication. Just a simple, "It's always nicer when we can meet in person, but we'll try to make this as close to that as we can," can help parents feel more comfortable and open. Take some time to acknowledge the challenges of Wi-Fi, sound issues, etc. Let them know if the virtual meeting cuts off, you'll call or text them (and be sure you have their phone number). Also, acknowledge the limitations of virtual meetings when it comes to privacy. Let them know up front if you are not in a private space, and ask about the location of their computer or phone. If you are having a sensitive conversation, and you need privacy, you'll need to share that with your parents, and kindly suggest that they ask others in the room to leave. And keep in mind, you may just have to make a phone call instead of speaking virtually in order to keep your conversation private.

Cameras

When it comes to using the cameras on your phone or laptop, I encourage you to turn yours on. It will help parents see your friendly smile, your open gestures, and your "I'm-interested-and-leaning-in" body language. But when it comes to your parents, allow them to make their own choice. It's just respectful.

Try to set up your computer where there's good lighting. Make sure you are centered on the screen. If there's too much room at the top of your shot, or on one side, it can feel uncomfortable and can distract from what you're saying.

It's hard to do, but when you're speaking or listening, try to look at the camera on your phone or computer and not your computer screen, at least for some of the conversation. Looking at the camera is the equivalent of eye contact. And if you're making eye contact, it can show you're listening. If that's hard for you to do, just explain to the parent you are looking at the screen instead of the camera so they won't think you're not listening.

One great thing about communicating virtually . . . it allows us to use all of the power of our nonverbal signs and signals to make connections and reinforce the power of our words.

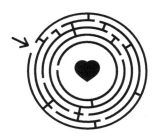

Challenging Conversations

If you're like most people, you don't look forward to challenging conversations. It's not fun to have to talk with a parent or caregiver when a student is struggling, but often you have to.

Why are these kinds of conversations so hard to handle? For starters, there's the possibility of causing a disagreement or argument. There's the possibility of bringing on strong, complex, and mixed emotions. There's an unpredictability to challenging conversations. They are hard to plan for. They are hard to control. And it's hard to predict an outcome.

So often, educators I work with call these conversations "difficult." But I say, they are only difficult if you frame them that way.

Instead, try to look at these conversations as opportunities. Opportunities to deepen your relationship with parents and caregivers, and opportunities to "test" yourself and your ability to use all that you know about communication to connect with others. When you do, you will look forward to these conversations not with that "pit-in-your-stomach" dread, but with a full heart, excitement, and an open mind.

Easy to say, hard to do, right? Well, here are some tips to help turn your dread into calm and confident anticipation.

One thing to note: Anytime you have to communicate something that is at all uncomfortable or challenging, try your best to deliver that news either face to face, virtually, or over the phone—not in a letter or email. Having challenging conversations is where you most need softer words and a gentle, reassuring tone that you can only communicate with your voice and body language.

If the information is time-sensitive, and you can't reach your parents even after leaving messages, there may be a time when you have to communicate through email or text. If that happens, be sure to read over what you write and think about all the ways parents might interpret your words to be sure your tone is spot-on: friendly, reassuring, and partner-like.

SETTING THE STAGE

Most importantly, and it probably goes without saying, challenging conversations are easier to have if you don't go into them "cold." Taking a few minutes to prepare can make all the difference.

The best way to lay the groundwork for challenging conversations is to get ahead of them by building relationships with parents at the start of the year. You can do this by making "relationship-building" home visits, initiating positive phone calls, chatting parents up at "Back-to-School Nights" . . . reaching out in any way will communicate that you are both on the same team and that you see the beauty in their child. Your challenging conversations will be that much more challenging if the first time parents hear from you is when there's something negative to discuss.

Put on Your Thinking Brain

Spend some time thinking about the parent or caregiver you'll be talking with. Do you know them? Is there already a relationship? If this is the first time you're communicating with them, ask yourself, *What else could be going on in their lives?* That will help you think about your approach.

It may also get you thinking . . . *Am I the right person for this conversation?* There may be another staff person in the building that has a closer relationship with the parent or caregiver who would be a better fit for delivering the news, or might just be able to join you and the parents during the conversation to help it go smoothly. If that's not possible, at the very least, that staff person might be able to give you more information or pointers about the family before the meeting that will help you approach the conversation in a calm, reassuring way.

One thing to note: Try to avoid a situation where there are lots of staff members in the room and only one parent. This can create a power dynamic that can leave a parent feeling outnumbered, overwhelmed, and defensive. If other staff will be present, make sure the parent knows ahead of time who will be in the room so they don't walk in and immediately feel surprised and uncomfortable.

Next, choose the right time and place—a time and place that works for the parent. The goal is to make them feel as comfortable as possible. Try to avoid at all costs having a conversation with a parent in the middle of the lobby(!) or at the end of their double shift. Let them tell you what works best for them. As hard as it is for you to deliver the news, it will be harder for them to receive it, so try to make them as comfortable as possible.

Review some of my tips from the previous chapter, "The Nuances of Tone and Body Language," on being welcoming, striking a partnership tone, and using your body language to be reassuring. And don't forget about the coffee!

Conversation Goals

Prepare by thinking about two or three clear goals for your conversation. You want to inform the parent, come to an agreement, and offer support. And spend time thinking about what I call "specific generalities." You'll want to paint with broad strokes when you are laying out your concerns. You won't want to get down in the weeds of specific things that might have happened, because this has the potential to create conflict.

Do a Self Check-In

Next, identify your emotional state. Think about what a parent could say that might trigger you. Clear your assumptions. If you think there's the possibility you might get worked up in the conversation, you may even want to write down "I will" or "I won't" statements like these:

"I will stay calm."
"I will remember that this parent loves their child."
"If I feel myself getting emotional, I will take a breath."
"I won't take this personally."
"I won't raise my voice."
"I won't lose my patience."

Writing down the actual words can be a powerful exercise that can help in emotional conversations.

THE CONVERSATION

Before you begin, remember to breathe! Deep, slow breaths will help you center yourself and help you find your calm. And remember, it's a conversation, not a lecture. What you're really hoping for is a dialogue.

Get to the Point

Be brief. Outline the issue (using your "specific generalities"), and ask your parents for help or for more information. This immediately includes them in the solution.

> *"Tell me, how are things going at home?"*
>
> *"I don't know the answer. Can you help me understand the best approach for your child?"*

Getting to the partnership piece of the conversation as early as possible will help you get to solutions quicker.

Avoid "Loaded" Words

In broadcasting, I learned there's a big difference between the words "says" and "claims." When you lay out concerns, use neutral language. You are just presenting the facts, not passing judgment. Don't make it personal. And change your "I" to a "we." Avoid using "you," as in "you need to…." or "you didn't…." That will shut down the conversation pretty quickly, or worse yet, escalate it in a negative direction. And include information that is positive. This will remind the parent that you see their whole child.

Don't Pile On

Leave some things unsaid. This is not the time for you to reach back to every negative encounter you have had with the student. This conversation is not about you unloading all of your frustrations. It's about reaching out for help from the person who knows the child best.

Practice Active Listening

Speak slowly and softly and ask lots of open-ended questions. Dig deeper. This means avoiding "yes" or "no" questions. Relax and let the conversation breathe. Give the impression that you'll stay as long as you need to find solutions. Listen more than you talk. Try not to interrupt your parent, and agree and affirm what they're saying often. A quick, "I love that you noticed that," or "I think you are exactly right," or "great idea" (even if you've already thought of it). This will give them the confidence to keep talking. Be mindful of your body language and keep your reactions empathetic.

What if you've done all these things and your parents still get angry or defensive? Well, don't respond with anger. Recognize that these strong emotions are not about you. They come from a place of love. And remember, it's not about you being "right." This may mean you'll have to apologize, or possibly even accept responsibility for something. That's okay. Don't forget that your goal is to do what you need in order to get to a place of partnership that's good for your student.

If the meeting is getting emotional, soften your tone and voice even more. Mirror back what you're hearing from the parents: "Just so I understand . . . ." Acknowledge what they are saying and acknowledge their anger. You may even have to take a break. "I feel myself getting a little emotional, so I'm going to excuse myself for moment." And if you have to, just agree to postpone the discussion for another time. This will give you and your parents time to think and work through their strong emotions.

When we practice active listening, our words, tone, and body language can work together to demonstrate that we respect and value our families.

WRAPPING IT UP, NOT SHUTTING IT DOWN

At this point, you'll want to ask some closed-ended questions. You'll want to make sure you've worked out a clear plan for moving forward. Agree to keep the lines of communication open. Check to make sure parents have been heard and let them know that this won't be your last contact with them. Suggest a time to check back in to gauge their child's progress. Here are some ways you can do that:

> *"Are we good?"*
> *"Do you feel comfortable with our plan?"*

"Is there anything we're missing that might help?"
"Let's touch base in a few weeks to see how things are going."

Also, acknowledge the expertise the parent brought to the conversation and make sure they know you value them:

"It's always so helpful to talk with you."
"You really know your child and you have some great ideas and insight."
" I really value your input. It takes both of us working together to help your student succeed."

Finally, thank the parent for coming in and taking the time to meet. Or taking the time to talk over the phone. And make sure your thank-you is sincere.

After the conversation, don't forget to reflect on how it went and how you handled it. Jot down some quick notes if you think that will help you prepare for the next challenging conversation you have. The more you can reflect, the more comfortable you'll be moving forward.

That's it! I know it's hard. But if you can get to a place where you feel prepared and ready for these conversations, you may even get to a place where you look forward to them. They are a chance for you to grow and learn and become a better communicator and maybe . . . even a better person.

Dishing Out Data

This is a book for educators, so I feel compelled to include a separate chapter on academic data and the best way to communicate to parents both the data and its meaning. But really, academic data is just like any other information we want to share with parents.

Statistics, both qualitative and quantitative, do present a lot of unique challenges because the world of data and data collection seems to be particularly full of complicated terms, confusing acronyms, and incomprehensible graphs and charts. But the bottom line is: parents and caregivers can understand data, test scores, standards—all of it—but only if we follow the communication principles outlined in this book, and if we take the time to present the data in a way they can understand.

SHARING IS CARING

Sharing data with parents is important. In education, the data in standardized tests and assessments often drives instruction. Data can also show exactly where students may be struggling, exactly what they need to work on, and exactly where they are making progress. This can be more helpful information for parents than grades on tests and homework. That's why it's important to make the effort to have conversations and communications around data.

The following sections provide tips on how to have meaningful conversations with parents around data.

Use Your Words

Read over the data report you want to share with a parent. Then put it away where you can't see it. This is key. Don't keep the report in front of you, or you will be tempted to use the language of the person who wrote the report which, I'm willing to bet, was written in "educationese."

After you've put it down, think about it. Think about what it shows and what it means. Then write or tell someone what it says. Pretend you're sharing it with just one person, your mother or best friend, someone who doesn't have a background in education. And pretend you can share it only once. That will help you get to what is really important.

This step is crucial. You have to make sure you have processed and understood the data before you can share it with someone else. You have to understand all of it before you decide what is important to share with a parent.

As a reporter, I sometimes had to cover medical stories. Obviously, I am not a doctor and have limited medical training. If the medical story was on, let's say, a procedure, I always asked lots and lots of questions before the on-camera interview began. My goal was to kind of become an "expert" in the procedure. Once I understood everything about the procedure, I could decide what information I needed to share with viewers, and what details I could leave out.

Which brings up my next point.

Divvy Up the Data into Key Points

Remember the Rule of Three from Chapter 5 when I stressed using the three main points that viewers needed to know? Take the same approach. Ask yourself: *What are the three points my parent needs to know?* And then think about how to share those three ideas in simple ways, using simple words.

Your three points might not even be the same for different students, depending on what the data shows. Remember, parents may come into conversations about data already intimidated. You don't want to give them information overload and scare them off.

After you've shared your three points, parents may ask questions, and you can pass along more details or more information . . . you can layer them in slowly. But even if parents don't ask more questions, you've hit the highlights, and hopefully, left them with enough information that they have something to celebrate with their children, or suggestions on how they can work with their children to improve.

It's All about Context

I can remember years ago when my son's school sent home a little half sheet of paper along with his standardized test scores. And let me just say that it's a wonder the paper made it home in his messy backpack! Anyway, the paper had a three-digit number on it (728), and it also indicated he was in the "Pass Plus" range, whatever that was. All of this was great to know, but the paper left me wondering, 728 out of what? What did Pass Plus even mean? To me, it seemed the school was checking off the box, "Shared data with parents," without providing the information I wanted and needed to truly understand the numbers. I wanted and needed to know what the test was for, the scoring range, and what Pass Plus meant. But without all of that information, the numbers were meaningless.

It's sort of like going to the doctor, and she takes some blood tests and gives you the numbers. "Your ratio was 141 to 53." Okay, great, but what does that mean? Is it normal? concerning? low? Without the follow-up explanation, "Normal is 130-150 over 50, so you're normal," the numbers are nice, but mean nothing to you.

If need be, take the time to come up with a "key" to the numbers for parents, like a map key. And keep the key simple and easy to understand. It's okay if you don't include all the information. Just use simple definitions, simple test score ranges, enough of an explanation for parents to make sense of the data, and enough information for them to gauge where their children are, compared with where they should aim to be.

Think about What the Data Means

You've shared the test scores or the reading level, and you've worked with the parent to put it into context. Now take some time to share with the parent what the data means, what it can indicate, and what it suggests are ways to address any problems. It means the student is not reading at grade level. It means they need to work in these three areas. It means they are on track to graduating and passing their end-of-course assessments. By knowing what the data means, parents can fully participate in the process of coming up with ideas and finding solutions to help their children succeed.

If you're struggling to explain to a parent what the data means, remember why you gave the assessment or test in the first place. That should help you understand how to interpret the scores. Or ask a colleague how they explain it to parents.

Remember to present the information to parents in a way that is factual and not judgmental. If the data isn't encouraging, you don't want parents to feel they are to blame.

NOW TALK IT THROUGH

Explaining and interpreting data is important, but it's the conversation that follows that's so very, very powerful. Why? Because it's "the money moment!" That is, these conversations are where parents will really be able to bring their expertise about their child to the table. There may be things going on at home that you know nothing about; you may learn things about the child that you never knew. Talking through the data together gives a parent a chance to share and explain. The parent's perspective in interpreting the data is invaluable, and will help you support the child in the classroom. And your perspective will help the parent support the child at home. It's also a great chance for parents to ask questions.

What if a parent doesn't ask questions? Well, grease the wheel by asking some yourself! If the student is doing well, ask the parent, "What have you been working on at home?" If the student is not doing so well, ask, "Is there some way you think I might support him?" Or "How does she learn best?" Those are two very powerful openings that might get the parent thinking and talking. And if you think the parent might not feel comfortable asking questions, share the questions other parents have asked before. You can say, "A lot of parents wonder about how hard it is to move up in the scoring range, well . . . ." Or remark, "Another parent asked about how this related to whether or not their child moved on to the next grade . . . ." You can take the pressure off a shy or intimidated parent by sharing what you know are common questions.

Once parents understand the data, the next step is developing a plan based on the data.

LEAVE WITH TO-DO LISTS AND CLEAR-CUT GOALS

Think about the earlier example where the doctor gave you blood tests and some numbers. You have the information and now you know what it means. The question is: what do you do about it? If your test results are normal, the doctor may tell you to keep on doing what you're doing. If your numbers are high, she may tell you to watch what you eat; if they're low, she might prescribe medicine. She's leaving you with action you need to take based on the data.

Now it's time to work with parents so that both you and the parents can do something with the information from the data. Think of it from the parents' perspective: "It's great that you shared where my child is with his reading scores, but what do I need to do to help him improve?"

Before you offer parents action items, take some time to discuss and set some clear, realistic goals for the student, both short-term and long-term. It's important to set goals together. If the parent is at the table helping to develop the goals and the steps to achieve them, the parent can give you deeper insight into their child and how he learns. And the parent is more likely to buy into the plan and take ownership. Which means it's more likely the plan will work.

After you work together to set goals, offer up how you will help the student.

"I will keep a closer eye on how he is doing."

"I will be changing my approach to working with him to include a different way of teaching the information."

"I will be including him in a small group of kids who are also doing well, and asking them to work on an activity to build on the lesson and take the learning to a higher level."

This shows you will have some skin in the game, and parents will appreciate it.

After you've shared your action plan, it's time to offer parents some suggestions:

"So that's what I plan to do . . . it would be great if you could support this at home by . . . ."

When you offer suggestions, make sure they're doable and talk through them with parents. But make sure they get to choose how to help. Don't tell them what to do; instead, coach them just as you would coach a student. Help them set their own goals based on what will work in their lives. Sure, we want parents to read to their kids every night for 30 minutes, but let's be real, that's not doable for many of our parents. Instead, work with them to set a goal of reading two nights a week.

Make sure you offer parents more than one option for supporting learning at home. Perhaps reading at night isn't possible, but maybe working literacy skills into the drive to school is: "Look at that big red sign. What are the letters on that big red sign?" Maybe for some parents, reading activities won't work at all, and they may choose to support learning at home simply by stressing the importance of reading and reinforcing our efforts at school. You can work with them to develop a list of things to say to their child like: "I love it that you love books," or "Did you do your reading homework tonight?" If we let parents choose how they think they can best support learning, they will be more likely to buy into the idea, own the action, and be successful.

Be specific. For example, if a child is struggling in fluency, give the parent some specific ways to work on fluency.

And remember, when the student achieves the goals, celebrate the team effort together—and don't forget to include the student!

FOLLOW THROUGH AND FOLLOW UP

Follow-up meetings are simple enough, and keep the work moving forward. They're also good times to discuss what's working and what isn't and good opportunities for both you and your parents to work through obstacles, adjust goals, and refine or build on your to-do lists. And it gives you another chance to continue to build and maintain your relationships.

WORDS OF ENCOURAGEMENT

Being encouraging is especially important if you're sharing information or data that might be troubling for parents. Hopefully, you've already taken some time to build a relationship with them, and they're open to information and aren't defensive. Now's the time for you to shine, to show your confidence in your ability to work with the student in the areas where you need to. And now's the time to show your confidence in the parents' ability not only to understand the data, but also to support the work at home.

As you begin to share data, call on your teaching skills. Most of this information will be new material for parents, and you'll have to present it a few different ways. Maybe you'll have to find new ways to explain something, maybe you'll have to explain it a few different times, or even draw a picture. You may have to teach or model the skills that parents need in order to help their children at home. But don't doubt that parents can understand the data. How will you know when they do? It's easy. You'll see the same lightbulb in their eyes that you see in your students' eyes when they understand what you're teaching.

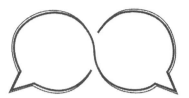

Making Good on Closing the Communication Loop

You've already taken the first step to getting good at all this communication stuff. You probably have already developed an awareness that you didn't have before, and maybe you'll never look at your school newsletter the same way.

That's a good thing. But the best way to get good at being conversational is to practice. When I was a budding broadcaster, I used to rip articles out of the newspaper and rewrite them into broadcast form just for practice.

I'm not suggesting you do that, but the more you can practice, the more you will get it. Engage parents in conversations, and ask for their feedback. And then accept the constructive feedback and build it into your next exchange.

When (preferably before) your school sends out a communication, read it over and as you do, think about how it reads, and what it says from the perspective of a parent or someone outside the education bubble. Is it conversational? Is it warm? Does it give just the right amount of information? Does it use plain language?

Spend a little extra time on your writing and on your emails. Use a thesaurus to look up simpler words if you need to. Then read what you've written through a critical lens.

ASSESS HOW YOU WRITE TO PARENTS

As you read over your writing, here are some other tricks and techniques from the world of broadcasting that you can use, and some of the major points you should keep in mind when you're using your critical lens.

Out Loud and Proud

Read what you've written out loud. This is the most important thing you can do. By reading your work out loud, you will catch clumsy language and sentence structure, and you'll hear the big words and acronyms. This practice will also help you as you hold conversations with parents. You'll come to know what words are truly conversational, and what words are not. You'll also hear when your writing has too many details or is overly wordy—and who knows, maybe you'll simply run out of breath if your sentence structure is too complicated!

When you read your work out loud, you can also work on your tone and switch up which words you're stressing. You'll hear how certain words might be interpreted, and you can rewrite to clarify or soften up the language, if you need to.

Check the Reading Level

In case you didn't know, when you write a letter or email (or really any document), there are readability tools that you can use to review the reading level of your work. With these tools, you highlight words, passages, or documents, and the program tells you what reading level those words, passages, or documents are, whether they're a typical eighth-grade reading level, or a second-grade level, and so on. These programs are different, so contact a colleague or do an internet search to learn how to do a reading-level check in the program you're using.

When you use the tool, don't just check the level of the entire letter or flyer because this computes the average reading level for the entire document. You want to make sure your families understand every word. Instead, check each paragraph, maybe even each sentence. This way, if the words in a paragraph or sentence are too complicated, you can rewrite that paragraph or sentence.

And remember, in broadcasting, we were told to aim for a fourth- to sixth-grade reading level. If you write at that level, most everyone will be able to understand.

Note: If you search online for resources and websites to recommend to parents, make sure you read those over through the lens of your newfound awareness.

There's lots of stuff out there, but it's not always written in plain language and in a clear, respectful way. Some resources may need a rewrite. As mentioned earlier, you don't want to give too many references, and you don't want to recommend resources or sites that parents might find frustrating or unfriendly.

Think about the Content

When you review your writing, along with being aware of the language you're using, double-check the content from another standpoint. Can you explain the purpose for the communication in one sentence? Are there more than three or four points? Is what you've written overwhelming or too long? Did you include the information parents really need to know? Did you include "the why"? Does what you've written appeal to the parents' emotions? Does it include something the parents can do to help? Finally, did you acknowledge the parents' expertise with a respectful "thank-you"?

Every letter, every communication I write, ends with, "Thank you for all you do to support your child's learning." It's a little thing, but I think it's important.

Check for Unanswered Questions

Perhaps I can explain this one best with the help of a little test. Read this television story from a few years ago. As you do, think to yourself, *what questions do I have?*

> *Indiana University is no longer the number one party school in the nation. The Princeton Review released its rankings today. The survey ranked IU number one last year and that was a source of stress for many at the University.*

Good news for IU right? But this story left you wanting more, didn't it? Because if IU isn't number one, which school is? (Even though it's been a few years, I still wanna know)!

There's obviously a big unanswered question here, and sometimes when we talk with or write to parents, we also leave unanswered questions. When you write something for your parents, be sure to read it over and think, *what questions would I have as a parent? What questions will my parents think and feel after reading this?* We don't want them to have to take the extra step of making a follow-up phone call, or sending a follow-up text or email, because maybe they won't—and then you've lost them. Make it as easy as possible by giving them what they need to know in the first place.

Don't Take That Tone with Me!

Ask yourself: *is what I've written respectful? Does it convey that my parents and I are in a partnership? Does it acknowledge the value of parents and welcome their input? Is it friendly, or is it authoritative? Can a different word soften what I've said or written?* And as you check for tone, think about where the parents are coming from, how they might interpret what you've said or written based on where, emotionally, they might be that day.

ARE YOU CLOSING THE COMMUNICATION LOOP?

As you reflect on your conversations with parents, here are some more tricks and techniques from the broadcast world that you can use, and some of the major points you should keep in mind.

The "Best Friend" Test

In broadcasting, we check our communications using what we call the "best friend" test. The idea is that you should communicate to the viewer in the same way that you would communicate with your best friend over a cup of coffee or a glass of wine. The "best friend" test is a good way to measure clear, concise, and conversational English.

Here's an example: Would you say to your best friend, "Saint Joe Police arrested 33-year-old Joe Smith for the Moto-Mart robbery on October 26." Probably not. But you might say, "Hey, did you hear the police made an arrest in yesterday's convenience store robbery?" It's much more conversational. If you take out the "Hey, did you hear," you have a news story: "Police made an arrest in yesterday's convenience store robbery." Neat huh?

So as you think about your conversations with parents, think about how you would convey the information to your best friend, one who's not in education. It will help put you in a casual, conversational frame of mind and help you use simple language and a friendly, open tone. It will also help you pare down your information.

Check for Understanding

Parents may not like a decision or a policy you have to make, but you always want them to leave with understanding and knowledge. When you speak with parents, ask if they have questions, and maybe even gauge where they are through their body language.

If a parent does ask a question, make sure you let the parent know you value that question. Simply saying "Good question!" can help build the relationship with that parent by bolstering their self-esteem and confidence. It also communicates an atmosphere of openness that can encourage other parents to ask questions.

Don't take it personally when parents have questions. It means they've really listened.

Questions and Concerns: Anticipate, Anticipate

Keep in mind, even if you show you're open to questions, and even ask if there are questions, sometimes your parents will not speak up, and they will not let you know they don't understand.

So before you have your conversations with parents, try your best to think through all the possible angles and questions you're likely to get from parents about the information you're trying to communicate. Put yourself in your "best friend" shoes, and anticipate questions and concerns.

Instant Replay

Spend some time replaying and reflecting on conversations you've had. Ask yourself: *If I had to do it again, what could I have phrased better? How could I have used more partnership language? What did my body language convey?* Thinking about the words you used, and the way you used them, as well as how they were received, will help you improve future conversations.

OTHER WAYS TO IMPROVE YOUR COMMUNICATIONS

Sometimes it's hard to adopt an outsider's point of view and see just where you need to improve. Reaching out to others for a fresh perspective can help with your writing and your language.

Engage Others in This Work

Who would be better to tell you if what you're saying or writing makes sense than your students' parents? Think about asking a few of them to read over your presentations or your letters before you send them out. Then ask them what they understood and what they didn't. Also ask them what other questions they have after reading it. They can serve as your best resource. A word of caution: it's important to ask more than one parent so that you get a more complete picture of your communications.

You might also think about working with your school's community partners like your afterschool program providers, student mentors, or youth development leaders. They bring an outside perspective and, as your partners, already support your goals. Perhaps Girl Scouts run an after-school program in your school, or maybe your school has a close relationship with a local church. Ask volunteers from partnering organizations like these to look over your communications, and ask them what they don't understand. They may have a bit more knowledge about your school, but they aren't in the education bubble and will still be able to provide you with the feedback you need to improve.

Looking at all of your communications could also be a great project for your school's PTA or PTO. Think of the potential for building relationships with an entire group of active and engaged parents!

Engaging parents and community partners in this work is a win-win. It will help your parents and community partners feel more respected and appreciated and part of the process. It will also help you. Those parents and partners will have a greater understanding that they can then share with other parents. They'll also see your commitment to them and your students and school, firsthand. You'll be creating champions on lots of levels.

And one more idea. As I started this work in my district, I reached out to all of my friends from the "biz"—former journalists from our local television stations. I also recruited journalism and writing professors, and I talked them into helping me write parent communications. We worked as a team to help draft letters and decode acronyms. My reporter friends and colleagues loved being somewhat on the "inside" of the school district, and they loved putting their expertise to use for such a good cause.

There's no reason you, too, can't reach out to your television station or university to do the same. Even if they don't write for you, they might be able to edit what you've put together, or serve as an informal focus group to help you figure out information your parents need.

Use a "Closing the Loop" Checklist

Whether you're working by yourself or with a team, keep this communication checklist handy to remind you of all the different principles of effective communication you've learned.

- ☐ My communication had a definite purpose.
- ☐ I had a certain parent or family in mind when creating the communication.
- ☐ I cleared my mind of assumptions about my parents and families.
- ☐ I thought about the emotional state of my parents and families.
- ☐ My tone reflected partnership.
- ☐ I arranged my ideas in a logical order.
- ☐ I only included "need-to-know" facts.
- ☐ I left out unnecessary details.
- ☐ I included background information and did not assume knowledge.
- ☐ I included "the why."
- ☐ I left no unanswered questions.
- ☐ I used effective examples.
- ☐ I used partnership language.
- ☐ I included an "ask."
- ☐ I used "You" and "I" and "We."
- ☐ I was aware of "The Rule of Three."
- ☐ I used an active voice.
- ☐ I used simple sentences and plain language.
- ☐ I included only one fact per sentence, as often as possible.
- ☐ I avoided acronyms.
- ☐ I avoided "five-dollar" words.
- ☐ I used simple words.
- ☐ I read my communication out loud.
- ☐ I was aware of my body language.
- ☐ My body language was open and accepting.
- ☐ I invited questions from my parents and families.
- ☐ My parents and families demonstrated with their questions and body language that they were engaged.
- ☐ I checked in to make sure my parents and families understood.
- ☐ I thanked my parents and families.
- ☐ I reflected on my communication.

Putting It All Together

The more you are aware, the more you will learn, and the more your thought processes will begin to change. In order to get you thinking, here's an example of what was going through my mind when I worked on a short communication for parents.

I was asked to rewrite a recorded phone message for parents about their students' standardized test scores. The message included all kinds of facts: dates, phone numbers, names of district offices, etc. It was long and included a lot of information.

Here is the original message:

Hello. This is a message from the school district. If your child took the ISTEP test in Indiana last year, within the next few days, you should receive a letter from the Indiana Department of Education regarding how to see your child's scores from last spring's testing. This is an important notification, as not only will you be able to see your child's scores now, but from November 9 to November 13" you will be able to request that the state rescore your child's test, if you feel it should be. Unlike past years, the school cannot make the request.

You are the only person who can do this. You may wish to have portions of your child's test rescored if the score is very close to the passing range, or if you believe they may have actually done better on the test than the score reflects. This does not apply to those students scoring in the Pass+ range. The letter you will receive contains your code that will give you access to your child's results. You will not receive your child's scores in this letter—only by using this code to access the State's Parent Network website. Please follow directions on how to log in beginning on Monday, November 9. All requests for rescoring must be made by Friday, November 13. Unfortunately, the state will not accept any requests after this date. If you have any questions, or if you do not receive your letter by this Friday, please call your school principal or the district at XXX-XXX-XXXX.

This is an important communication with lots of good information that the school district needs to share. Frankly, lots and lots of information, period.

I rewrote the script to say:

Hello. This is an important message from the school district about your child's test scores. If your child took ISTEP last year, be on the lookout for a letter from the Indiana Department of Education. You should get it in the mail in the next few days.

This letter is very important. It has information you need to log onto the state education website to see your child's test scores.

The scores will be posted on Monday and it's important to log on and check the scores right away. If your child is close to passing, you will want to ask the state to regrade his or her test again. You can do this online. But, you will only have five days to make the request. The deadline to have your child's test regraded is this coming Friday, November 13. If you miss the deadline, the state will not regrade the test. You are the only person who can ask for a regrade; schools are not allowed to make the request.

If you need help logging onto the state education website to see the grades, or if you have questions or concerns about the scores, please call your school as soon as possible. Also, if you do not receive your letter by tomorrow, call the school.

So what did I do here? First, I started by thinking about the purpose of the communication. The purpose of this recorded phone message was to let parents know they would be getting a really important letter.

It's that simple.

But in sending the phone message, the school district also had a chance to include a little more information. So I also included information about the rescoring.

Including the information about the test scores and the rescoring was part of the overall strategy around the phone message. This was the first time parents heard about the rescoring process. They may not have retained the information, but it was important for them to at least hear about the process. They would be exposed to information about the rescoring process a second time when they read the letter, and they would hear about it again when the school called to check whether they requested a rescore.

There you have it. These three communications—a recorded phone message, a letter, and a follow-up call—gave us our best chance of reaching our parents. We also planned to get the word out through the news and social media, so if parents heard or read about it that way, that was a bonus.

Now, let's go through the following exercise line by line.

> First, I moved the word "important" up to the opening sentence, and included "your child's test scores."

This was designed to get parents' attention. If I'm a parent and I'm making dinner or driving when I get your phone call, I'm not really focused. If you begin with, "Hello. This is a message from the school district," I'm going to hang up.

But if you were to say, "It's important" and "it's about your child's test scores," you would have my attention, or you'd have a better chance of getting it. I care about my child's test scores, even if I'm making dinner.

Next, I wrote:

> *If your child took the ISTEP test last year . . .*

This message went to all parents. If your child didn't take the test, I was telling you that you didn't have to pay attention. That wasn't ideal; we'd like all parents to know such information. But the intention behind this sentence was to make parents perk up even more, and think: *Oh, that's me . . . my child took it!* And then they'd listen even more closely to the message.

The recorded message continued:

Be on the lookout for a letter from the Indiana Department of Education.

Active voice, conversational writing, and an "ask." Bingo. I chose to include the formal name of the Indiana Department of Education, instead of shortening it to "the state," because the formal name was on the letter's return address. Also, maybe parents were receiving other letters from "the state," and we wanted them to pay special attention to this one.

Then I told them when to expect the letter:

You should get it in the mail in the next few days.

There you go. If parents hung up after the first ten seconds, they'd have the information I really needed to share.

But once I had their attention, I made the most of it by continuing:

It has the information you need to log on and check your child's test scores.

And right there, I answered the unanswered question: "Why is the letter important?"

The original version included all of the dates. I took those out, because let's face it, unless it's close to your birthday, you don't walk around really knowing the date—you just know if it's on a Monday or a Friday. Instead of dates, I wrote "in a few days" and "Monday and Friday." It's just the way people think.

The original version said:

You will be able to request that the state rescore your child's test, if you feel it should be.

As a parent, how would I know if it should be rescored? There's no guidance. The original went on to say:

You may wish to have portions of your child's test rescored if the score is very close to the passing range, or if you believe they may have actually done better on the test than the score reflects.

The fact of it was, if the student was close to passing, we, as a district, wanted that test rescored. I asked the parent to partner with us to ask for a rescore by writing:

If your child is close to passing, you will want to ask the state to regrade their test.

Notice that I called it "regrade" and not "rescore." In my opinion, "rescore" is a five-dollar word. Back in the day, when we were in school and thought our essay deserved a higher grade, we all walked into our classrooms to have our test regraded, right? Not "rescored." Better yet, I could have written, "have the state take another look at the test and grade it again," but hindsight is 20/20, right?

I also took out the part about the rescoring process not applying to Pass +. It's good information, but not necessary for this communication. To keep the phone message as simple as possible, I couldn't include everything, and I figured all of that information would be in the upcoming letter that I was telling parents to read.

So from a logical, linear progression of thought, what do you suppose the parents were thinking at that point?

How do I do that? How do I ask for a regrade?

And I answered that question:

You can do this online.

Again, I could have stopped there. If a parent were to hang up, I'd already given them all the important information. But I also wanted to impart a sense of urgency. That had to be the tone of this phone message. It was serious, important, and urgent. The original version read:

From November 9 to November 13 you will be able to request that the state rescore your child's test.

Again, including dates was wordy and not conversational. So I took those out. But the original version didn't convey a sense of urgency. Plus, had I said, "November 9 to November 13," I would not only be asking parents to pay attention to my important information, I would also be asking them to do a subtraction problem in their heads to figure out how much time they had to ask for a rescore. I could almost hear them doing the math: Put the thirteen before the nine and subtract.

And bang, I would've lost the parents. Instead, I wrote:

. . . you will only have five days to make the request.

Five days is not a long time, and parents were able to get a sense of the time frame. I drove the message home by repeating this information in another form, using the "Friday" reference, and I included the date only to avoid confusion about which Friday. Later in the communication, I talked about a Friday deadline for receipt of the letter. I could have taken the actual date out, but I wanted to be as clear as possible.

The deadline to have your child's test regraded is this coming Friday, November 13.

Notice that I also used the word "deadline," which signified it was urgent. It wasn't used in the original version, so there was no sense of urgency.

I went on:

If you miss the deadline, the state will not regrade the test.

That sounds scary and more urgent than the original wording:

Unfortunately, the state will not accept any requests after this date.

The original draft also spoke to "past years" . . .

> *Unlike past years, the school cannot make the request. You are the only person who can do this.*

In the interest of brevity and fulfilling the question: "what do they need to know" from this communication, I decided the "past years" part wasn't important, so I didn't include it. And although the rescore process had changed, not many parents knew what the process was in the first place, so they wouldn't even have had a reference for that change.

I also took out the references to the code that had been in the original:

> *The letter you will receive contains your code that will give you access to your child's results. You will not receive your child's scores in this letter—only by using this code to access the State's Parent Network website.*

Again, they will read that in the district's upcoming letter. The purpose of this phone message was to get them to read that letter and expose them to the basics of the process.

Instead of using "code," I wrote:

> *. . . contains information you need to log onto the IDOE website to see the scores.*

And I took out the details about the state's parent network. Again, that would all be in the letter.

Both the original and my version end with an offer to help. I chose to not include a phone number. Unless I repeated the number: *"That phone number again is . . . ,"* it would be useless. No one listens to an unscheduled, recorded message with a pen and paper in hand, ready to take down information and phone numbers.

I directed the parents who had questions to the school, instead of the district. We wanted them to have a relationship with the school, and to see the school as a resource. Plus, they likely already had the school's phone number.

That's how you put it all together.

Whew, that's a lot of information! Read both the original and my rewrite again, this time a little more closely.

When you look at the linear progression of information, you see that the first message jumped around a bit. Parents got information about when to request a re-score, before they got information about when they'd get the letter *and* before they got the information on the deadline. They got information about asking for a re-score—including dates—before they got information about when they might want to ask for a rescore. Do you get the picture? All the information was there (and then some), but it wasn't packaged in a digestible, understandable, or linear way.

When you think about tone, both communications were pretty equal in se-riousness, but the rewrite felt a little more urgent, and a little more like the way partners communicate; the rewrite reinforced that the school district and parents are partners.

When you think about the words, the second version had stronger, direct, and more active words.

And when you think about the amount of information, the rewrite was pretty straightforward, and was presented on a need-to-know basis. I also followed the Rule of Three: the first section of information was about the letter, the next was about the rescore process and deadlines, and the last section was about the offer for help.

Now read the revised version one more time. It seems effortless, but now you know how much thought went into each and every word, and into the placement of each and every sentence.

Ideas on Where to Begin

Okay. You've made it this far, and maybe you feel a little overwhelmed. You're probably thinking, *where do I begin?*

As I've said, you've already started—remember my former student, the oncologist? Just being in my class changed him, and made him aware of how he communicates with his patients. He says he no longer assumes that his patients bring any medical knowledge to their appointments, but he does respectfully acknowledge that they are the experts when it comes to their bodies. And he listens to them. Trust me, reading this book has already changed you.

You may be thinking, *but there is so much to this!* Well, let me stop here to point out that the overwhelming feeling you may be having is how many of our parents feel about our educational system and about helping their child. So I'll give you the same advice I would give a parent, just do one thing.

START SMALL

Setting small, achievable goals will allow you to gently and gradually change the way you communicate and the communications culture of your school. You will create champions as you build more meaningful relationships with parents.

And setting small, achievable goals will allow you to see progress and celebrate small successes throughout the year.

ENGAGE YOUR PARENTS

Don't forget, you're not alone. You can invite parents and community partners to help you with your communications. Here are some ways to go about that:

- **Ask your parents what they need you to work on first.** They can tell you what works for them and what doesn't. And they can help you prioritize your work. Or check with your school principal to see if your school or district surveys families (and I bet they do). If so, take a look at the questions and results. There might be information in there that can help inform your work. If there isn't, you might want to suggest a question or two that could be added to the survey, "How could our school home communication improve?" or "I understand the learning materials provided by the school." The more data or information you can pull from, the better. It will help you begin to see patterns that can form the basis of your work.
- **Set a goal of "two sets of eyes."** Create parent "editors" who review all the communications that go home using an "outsider-parental" lens. When it comes to writing and communications, two sets of eyes are always better than one.
- **Organize a volunteer communications team.** Invite writing and communication professionals and put together a team to help write and review communications. Not only can those professionals put their skills to good use, they will also love putting their skills to a new use.

START WITHIN

You can also begin to overhaul your own communications with families. Here are some ideas to help you improve your own practices.

- **Take a fresh approach to the new year.** No matter what may or may not have happened the previous year, or the year before, or what may or may not have happened to us in the past, there is a "fresh start" feeling in the first few weeks of school. Students are excited, staff seem rested and ready to go, and parents, too, are hopeful and engaged. Take advantage of this opportunity. Craft an engaging, warm welcome letter that is less about authoritative rules and procedures, and more about partnering with parents in the education of their children. Use a friendly tone and approach, and use simple words. Or change up your Open House spiel. Instead of the same old, "tell-your-child-to-go-to-bed-early-and-have-a-good-breakfast" mantra, take some time to ask parents what they did or didn't understand the previous year, or prepare simple handouts for parents on how they can help their kids at home. Or spend an hour or so crafting a warm "check-in" email and set it up in your email program to go out to parents, say once a quarter or every few weeks, or so. No "Dear Parents," or lengthy content. Just a quick, "Hi" or "Hello," and keep it short. It should feel exactly as though you were thinking of them and their child, and took a quick moment to let them know this. Because you *are* thinking of them and their child. You'll be surprised at how many parents will find reassurance in this simple effort on your part.

- **Revise mandatory communications which are sent to everyone.** Health forms, enrollment sheets, welcome letters, and so on—these are all opportunities for you to improve your connection with your parents and families. Underline cumbersome language and big words; think about the tone. If you don't have time to use your new skills to rewrite all of them, concentrate on friendly beginnings and endings, or make it a point to use friendly, partnership language moving forward. And boom, you've found a way to beat the time trap.

- **Assess your written communications.** It may be difficult to change some of the mandatory communications that your school sends out. So concentrate on your own outreach, instead; make sure your communications with parents are clear and understandable.

- **Rewrite standards.** Spend the year rewriting academic standards in ways that parents can understand. You can use this information in a variety of ways: on bulletin boards, hallway displays of student work, in newsletters, in text messages, and in letters sent home with your students. Once you've "translated" the standards, parents can begin to see how they can help.

- **Start with the most important things parents need to know.** Don't try to change everything at once. Instead, pick the top three things parents need to know for the year, which may vary by grade level. Do they need to understand the changes in the standards? Do they need to understand the one thing they can do to help support the work at home? Do they need to understand the college application process? And then concentrate on putting together the communication tools and pathways to reach out to the parents in those particular areas.

WORK WITH YOUR STAFF

It can also be powerful to work as a school or district to improve communications with families. A schoolwide or districtwide approach allows staff to learn from and support one another in the work. If you engage your staff in prioritizing the work, they'll be more likely to embrace it. Here are some ideas on how you might work as a staff to tackle communications. Again, just pick one.

- **Host a "coaching" session for the teachers and staff in your school.** I've talked about how simply raising awareness of the language we use can begin to change the ways we communicate. So make it a goal to raise awareness in your school or district. Share what you've learned with your staff. Once they begin to understand just how important words and conversations can be to building relationships with parents, there will be no going back.
- **Work with a team to conduct a communications audit.** Look at where you are right now with your communications . . . what works for parents and what misses the mark? Start by looking at your welcoming communications, and work your way up to challenging conversations. Identify strong communicators in your building or district and engage them in the effort.
- **Map existing communication pathways.** Work with your staff to discuss all the ways you reach out and communicate with parents. And discuss how those practices could be improved or expanded. This will help you begin to customize your content and conversations. More importantly, it will help you think about how and when parents receive information from you.

- **Concentrate on just one communication medium.** Work with staff to choose just one area where you'll work for the year. Perhaps say, "This is the year we'll get the website up to snuff, so let's review everything we include on our website, and make sure it's clear, respectful, and friendly." Or maybe, "Let's review all the writing in our newsletter and make sure it's what we want it to be and that it's helpful for parents." Or perhaps it's your Facebook messages. Choosing one area to focus on will allow you to divide the work into digestible pieces—and see your progress!
- **Start with ABC.** Ask your staff to make a list of the most common acronyms they use and spend the year crafting simple explanations of those acronyms. It will be good practice, and you can use your newly decoded language to put together "acronym-of-the-week" features for your website, newsletters, or Facebook posts.
- **Start with the "heavy hitters."** Make a list of the most common big words you use, and define or decode them as you did with acronyms.
- **Put together a couple of "scripts."** Talking points and scripts can help teachers and staff begin to have meaningful, clear conversations with parents. Sometimes it's hard to know how to begin, and it's hard to figure out how to handle certain conversations. Preparing scripts and even practicing conversations can help. If someone in your building happens to be especially good at conversations, ask that person to work with other staff or ask her to model during a staff meeting. Sometimes just seeing the possibilities can motivate change.

MEASURE YOUR PROGRESS

With all of these suggestions, decide how you will measure your progress. Perhaps there's a data point on communication or engagement in your family surveys. If not, you can add one, or you can create a parent focus group to help collect anecdotal evidence of your progress. Or maybe there's a data point on your teacher evaluation around communication. You could set some goals around that. Or maybe your school or district does schoolwide, family-friendly walk-throughs. You could look through those and see if there's data you can use to help you set some goals. I bet if you start looking, you'll find something you can use . . . because in the end, everything we do is about good communication.

Conclusion

In the end, it's important to remember that the responsibility for good, effective communication lies with us . . . with educators. It's our responsibility because it's easier for us to open up the lines of communication by reaching out to families than it is for them to overcome all of the communication barriers to reach us. It's our responsibility because we need to build relationships with families if we are to truly work in partnership to help students be successful, close the communication loop, and demonstrate that education belongs to all of us.

But look, this communication work, this relationship-building work is hard, and it takes time. And with everything else going on in education, it can be easy for it to get lost in all the other demands being made on your profession these days. I get it.

It can also get lost because these seem like such small things . . . changing a word here and there, lifting a brow or tilting a head, leaving out a detail and including a thank you. Kinda makes you wonder . . . *will it really make that much of a difference?* I think so, and I urge you to make some little changes and see for yourself. What do you have to lose? At the very least, you'll become better at crafting your Facebook and Twitter posts.

This book offers you the tools you need to be able to communicate with families. To be successful, you have to want to do it, you have to believe in your families, and you have to want to engage them. And when you close the communication loop, you also have to be ready and willing to open your heart and your mind, and listen to what families have to say. When you do, you may find that not only can you help kids succeed, you can enrich your life and change our world.

REFERENCES

Beebe, S. A., Beebe, S. J., & Redmond, M.V. (1996). *Interpersonal communication: Relating to others.* Allyn & Bacon.

Boulder Valley School District. (n.d.). *Parent Involvement.* https://www.bvsd.org/parents-students/get-involved

Chapman, A., & McCarthy, S. (2021, October 21). Reading body language signs and communications. *BusinessBalls.* https://www.businessballs.com/self-awareness/body-language/

Cherry, Kendra. (2021, October 21). Understanding body language and facial expressions. *Verywell Mind.* https://www.verywellmind.com/understand-body-language-and-facial-expressions-4147228

George Lucas Educational Foundation. Edutopia. (2015, April 7). *Sharing data to create stronger parent partnerships.* http://www.edutopia.org/practice/sharing-data-create-stronger-parent-partnerships

Henderson, A.T., & Mapp, K. L. (2002). *A new wave of evidence: The impact of school, family and community connections on student achievement.* Southwest Education Development Laboratory. https://sedl.org/connections/resources/evidence.pdf

Jenkins, R. (2014, August 14). The case for conversational writing. *Chronicle Vitae.* https://chroniclevitae.com/news/660-the-case-for-conversational-writing

King, S. (2000). *Stephen King on writing: A memoir of the craft.* Scribner.

Learning Heroes. (2020, May 19). *Parents 2020: COVID-19 closures: A redefining moment for students, parents, and schools.* https://r50gh2ss1ic2mww8s3uvjvq1-wpengine.netdna-ssl.com/wp-content/uploads/2020/11/LH_2020-Parent-Survey.pdf

Lechner, R. (2016). *Emergency closings FAQ.* Wilmette Public Schools. http://www.wilmette39.org/cms/one.aspx?portalid=360930&pageid=898908

Louisville Public Schools. (2016). *Louisville Public Schools Welcome Page.* http://www.lpslions.org/

Massachusetts Department of Elementary and Secondary Education. (2017). *Massachusetts model system for educator evaluation, appendix c: Teacher rubric.* http://www.doe.mass.edu/edeval/model/PartIII_AppxC.pdf

Mayer, R. E., Heiser, J., & Lonn, S. (2001). Cognitive constraints on multimedia learning: When presenting more material results in less understanding. *Journal of Educational Psychology, 93*(1), 187-198.

Meleen, Michele. *Examples of body language: recognize nonverbal cues.* Your Dictionary. https://examples.yourdictionary.com/examples-of-body-language.html

National PTA (2011, May 23). *National PTA, Harvard Family Research Project release issue brief on educating educators for meaningful family engagement* [Press release]. http://www.pwrnewmedia.com/2011/national_pta/educating_educators/

National School Public Relations Association. (2011, August 26). *National survey pinpoints communications preferences in school communications* [Press release]. http://www.nspra.org/files/docs/Release%20on%20CAP%20Survey.pdf

Navarro, J. (2009, October 28). The key to understanding body language: How our limbic brain helps us communicate honestly. *Psychology Today.* https://www.psychologytoday.com/blog/spycatcher/200910/the-key-understanding-body-language

Navarro, J. (2011, August 21). Body language basics: The honesty of body language. *Psychology Today.* https://www.psychologytoday.com/blog/spycatcher/201108/body-language-basics

Northampton Public Schools. (2016) *Our schools.* https://sites.google.com/a/northampton-k12.us/nps/our-schools

Parent Teacher Home Visits. (2018). *Educators and families on the same team for student success!* [Brochure]. https://iel.org/wp-content/uploads/2018/08/www.pthvp_.org_wp-content_uploads_2016_10_PTHV-digital.pdf

RTI Action Network. (2021). *What is response to intervention (RTI)?* http://www.rtinetwork.org/learn/what/whatisrti

Scottsdale Unified School District #48. (2016). *Gifted learning.* http://www.susd.org/index.php/programs/susd-gifted-learning

Strunk, W., & White, E. B. (1979). *The elements of style.* Macmillan.

Washoe County School District. (2016). *New vaccine requirement for students entering 7th grade.* www.washoeschools.net/Page/2890

NOTES

Made in the USA
Columbia, SC
30 August 2022

66355769R00076